W9-BCQ-831

SPECTRUM®

Reading

Grade 1

Spectrum®
An imprint of Carson-Dellosa Publishing LLC
P.O. Box 35665
Greensboro, NC 27425 USA

ISBN 978-0-7696-3861-4

12-140137811

Index of Skills

Reading Grade 1

Numerals indicate the exercise pages on which these skills appear.

Reading Comprehension

Comprehension Skills

Following directions—*All exercise pages*

Determining the main idea—51, 53, 55, 57, 59, 61, 63, 65, 67, 69, 71, 73, 75, 77, 79

Facts and details—55, 57, 59, 61, 63, 65, 67, 69, 71, 73, 75, 77, 79, 89, 91, 93, 95, 97, 99, 101, 103, 105, 107, 109, 111, 113, 115, 117, 119, 121, 123, 125, 127, 129, 131

Predicting outcomes—51, 53, 55, 57, 59, 61, 63, 65, 67, 69, 71, 73, 75, 77, 79

Sequencing events—3, 5, 7, 11, 25, 81

Classifying objects—15, 21, 49

Using the pictures 13, 21, 29, 31, 84

Phonics

Letters and Sounds

Letter study: 51, 53, 55, 57, 59, 61, 63, 65, 67, 69, 71, 73, 75, 77, 79

Blends—15, 17, 19, 23, 25, 27, 33, 51, 53, 55, 57, 80, 82, 83

Digraphs:

Ch–29   th–33   Ch, th, sh, wh–37
Sh–31   wh–35

Ending consonants—15, 17, 19, 21, 23, 25, 27, 82

Beginning consonants—3, 5, 7, 9, 11, 13

Long vowels—29, 31, 33, 35, 37, 39, 41, 43, 45, 47, 49

Short vowels—35, 37, 39, 41, 43, 45, 47, 49

Knowing the Words

Creating rhymes—9, 17, 27, 48, 51, 53, 55, 57, 63, 65, 77, 79, 87, 89, 91, 95, 97, 99, 101, 103, 105, 107, 109, 111, 113, 115, 117, 119, 121, 123, 125, 127, 129, 131

Sight word recognition—*All lessons*

Word recognition—*All lessons*

Choosing the correct word—61, 63, 65, 67, 73, 79, 81, 87, 89, 91, 93, 95, 97, 99, 101, 103, 105, 107, 109, 111, 123, 125, 132, 133, 137

Missing letters—51, 53, 55, 57, 59, 61, 69, 71, 75, 77, 113, 115, 135, 136

Learning to Study

Following directions—*All activity pages*

Note: If passages or directions are too difficult for the student, a teacher or parent should read them aloud to the student.

Table of Contents

Nonfiction: Due to content these pages have more advanced vocabulary. These passages may need to be read with a teacher or parent guide depending on child's reading level.

Little Duck

I think mama duk hers her egg hachin (handwritten)

What is that sound?

What do you think Mama Duck hears?

a duc (handwritten)

Something is saying, "Quack, Quack!"

What do you think is making that sound?

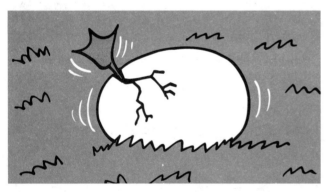

its a duc foot (handwritten)

That's a funny looking foot!

Whose foot do you think that belongs to?

the duc Hape (handwritten)

Hey, it's Little Duck!

How do you think Little Duck feels?

Picture Interpretation and Reading (for all stories): Introduce students to Little Duck, a sweet duckling who is the focus of the following stories. Suggest that the students look at the pictures and talk about what is happening. Have the students relate what they see to their own lives and experiences. Be aware of the vocabulary levels and needs of the group. Key words may be reinforced or developed by writing them on the board as each picture/picture scenario is discussed. First, have students read the story by themselves silently. Help students with any unfamiliar words. Next, have students read the story orally. Discussion questions have been provided to serve as a discussion guide.

Beautiful Beginnings

1.

2.

3.

Directions:

Beginning Consonants (1-2): Ask students to say each picture aloud and listen to the beginning sound. They then should write the beginning letter on the line below the picture.

Sequence (3): Have students look at all the pictures. Ask them to write **1** below the event that would happen first, **2** below the event that would happen second, and **3** below the event that would happen third.

Mama Duck

mecus she LiKs Little Duckle

Mama Duck kisses Little Duck on the head. "Hello, Little Duck," she says.

Why does Mama Duck kiss Little Duck?

Little Duck is hungs

"Are you hungry, Little Duck?" asks Mama Duck.

Does Little Duck look hungry?

it means i am hungry

Little Duck shakes his head up and down. Little Duck is hungry.

What does it mean when you shake your head up and down?

I Like to eat hotdogs

Mama Duck gives Little Duck some corn to eat.

What do you like to eat?

Name _____

Beautiful Beginnings

1.

f   f   s

2.

s   H   s

3.

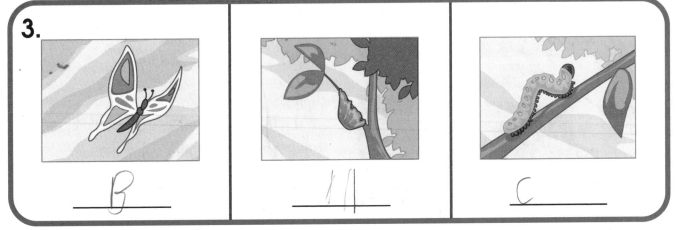

B   H   C

Directions:

Beginning Consonants (1-2): Ask students to say each picture aloud and listen to the beginning sound. They then should write the beginning letter on the line below the picture.

Sequence (3): Have students look at all the pictures. Ask them to write **1** below the event that would happen first, **2** below the event that would happen second, and **3** below the event that would happen third.

Wiggle-Waddle

she is fat.

Little Duck watches his mom walk. Mama Duck walks funny. She moves back and forth in a wiggle.

Why do you think Mama Duck walks that way?

He is arising.

Little Duck laughs. Why does his mom walk that way? Little Duck laughs and laughs.

Why is Little Duck laughing so hard?

Ba Keineath.

"What's so funny, Little Duck?" asks Mama Duck. "Ducks waddle. This is how we walk."

What does it mean to waddle?

Little Duck tries to walk like Mama Duck. He wiggles. He waddles. He wiggle-waddles. Little Duck walks like a duck. Mama Duck is happy.

Why is Mama Duck happy? How do you think Little Duck feels?

Little Duc

Beautiful Beginnings

1.

A _____ J _____ h _____

2.

L _____ L _____ t _____

3.

B _____ P _____ B _____

Directions:

Beginning Consonants (1-2): Ask students to say each picture aloud and listen to the beginning sound. They then should write the beginning letter on the line below the picture.

Sequence (3): Have the students look at all three pictures. Ask the students to write **1** below the event that would happen first, **2** below the event that would happen second, and **3** below the event that would happen third.

Dinnertime

toeechfish.

Little Duck follows his mom to the pond. The pond is very large.

Where is Little Duck going? Why do you think he is going there?

afishe.

Something moves in the pond. "What was that?" asks Little Duck.

What do you think moved in the pond?

he wifice it

"That's dinner!" says Mama Duck. Then, she quacks loudly.

What do you think will happen next?

wete

A small fish jumps high out of the water and splashes Little Duck.

How do you think Little Duck feels getting splashed?

Name _____

Beautiful Beginnings

1.

h _____   s _____   m _____

2.

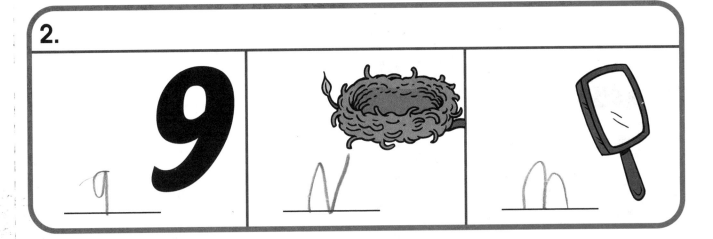

q _____   N _____   m _____

3.

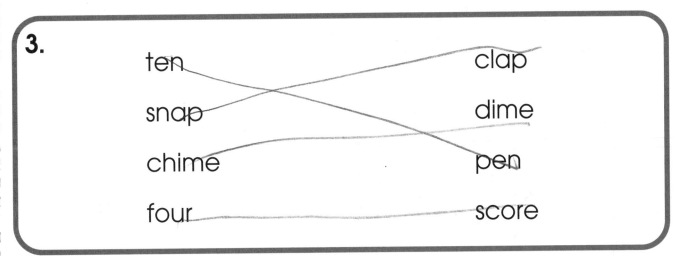

ten   clap

snap   dime

chime   pen

four   score

Directions:

Beginning Consonants (1-2): Ask students to say each picture aloud and listen to the beginning sound. They then should write the beginning letter on the line below the picture.

Rhyme Time (3): Have students draw lines connecting the words that rhyme.

Fish Is Not Dinner

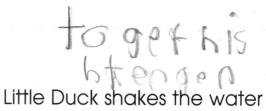

Little Duck shakes the water off his soft feathers. "Who are you?" asks Little Duck.

Why do you think the fish splashes Little Duck?

I feel bad.

"I am a fish, Little Duck. I swim in the pond. I am not dinner!"

How do you think the fish feels?

dinner

Mama Duck sees something. She waddles ahead. "Come along, Little Duck," she calls.

What do you think Mama Duck sees?

"Well, good-bye, fish," says Little Duck. "I guess we will eat something else for dinner."

Beautiful Beginnings

1.

2.

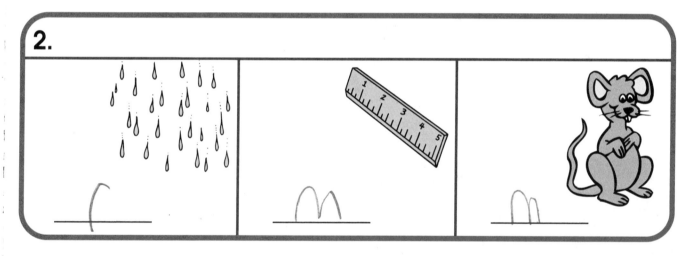

3.

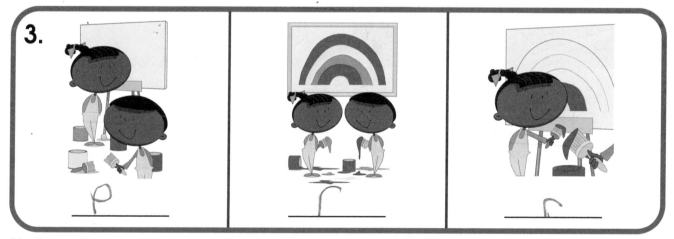

Directions:

Beginning Consonants (1-2): Ask students to say each picture aloud and listen to the beginning sound. They then should write the beginning letter on the line below the picture.

Sequence (3): Have your students look at all three pictures. Ask your students to write **1** below the event that would happen first, **2** below the event that would happen second, and **3** below the event that would happen third.

Make Way for Ducklings

Mama Duck walks to the edge of the road. Mama Duck turns her head both ways.

Why does Mama Duck do this?

"Cars make way for ducklings. Follow me, Little Duck," says Mama Duck.

What does Mama Duck mean?

Little Duck turns his head both ways like Mama Duck. Then, he follows Mama Duck across the road.

Why is it important to look both ways?

A boy sees the ducks crossing the road. He shouts, "Hey, make way for ducklings!" Little Duck crosses the road.

Do you think the boy is friendly? Why?

Beautiful Beginnings

1.

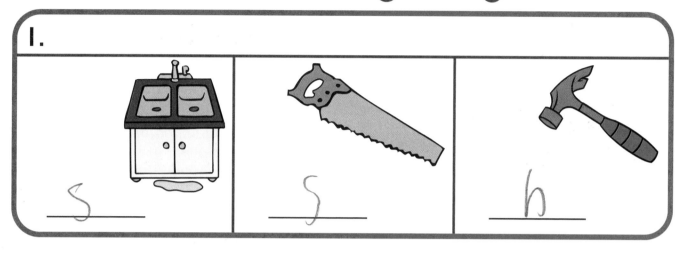

s _____ s _____ h _____

2.

t _____ c _____ t _____

3.

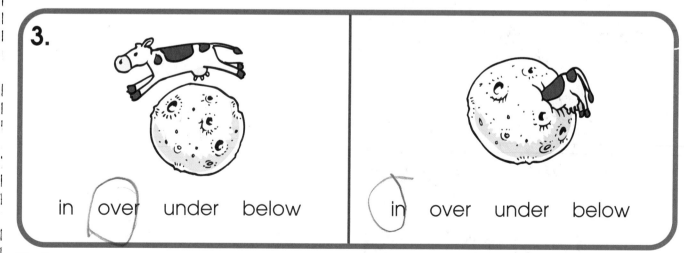

in (over) under below   (in) over under below

Directions:

Beginning Consonants (1-2): Ask students to say each picture aloud and listen to the beginning sound. They then should write the beginning letter on the line below the picture.

Using the Pictures (3): Have your students look at the pictures. Ask your students to circle the word that describes where the cow is located.

A Feast

pa farm

Little Duck follows Mama Duck up the hill. "Where are we going, Mama Duck?" asks Little Duck.

Where do you think they are going?

Yor + rde

"We are going to find some dinner. When the sun sets, it is dinnertime for people and for ducks," says Mama Duck.

What time do you eat dinner?

yes.

"Was fish our dinner?" asks Little Duck.

Do you like to eat fish for dinner?

yes

"Not tonight," answers Mama Duck. "Tonight, we have a feast!"

Do you know what a feast is?

Name _____

Exceptional Endings and Blends

1.

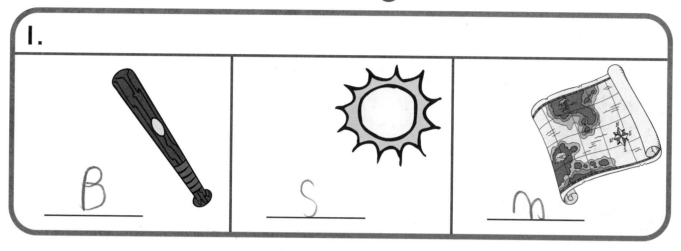

B _____   S _____   m _____

2.

S _____   f _____   t _____

3.

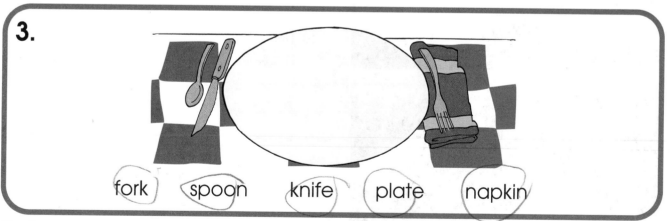

fork   spoon   knife   plate   napkin

Directions:

Ending Consonants (1): Ask students to say each picture aloud and listen to the ending sound. They then should write the ending letter on the line below the picture.

Blends (2): Ask students to say each picture aloud and listen to the beginning sound. They then should write the beginning blend on the line below the picture.

We Go Together (classification) (3): Have students circle the words of the set of three things that go together.

Bread Crumbs

Ke8

"What is a feast?" asks Little Duck.

Can feasts be different for different people?

Seds

"A feast is a large dinner. Tonight, we are eating something special," says Mama Duck.

What do you think Mama Duck and Little Duck will eat?

fish

"Does it taste like fish?" asks Little Duck.

What would you like to eat at your own feast?

Kes

"It tastes better than fish. Tonight, we're having bread crumbs!" she says.

Would you like to eat bread crumbs? Why or why not?

Exceptional Endings and Blends

1.

b _____   p _____   p _____

2.

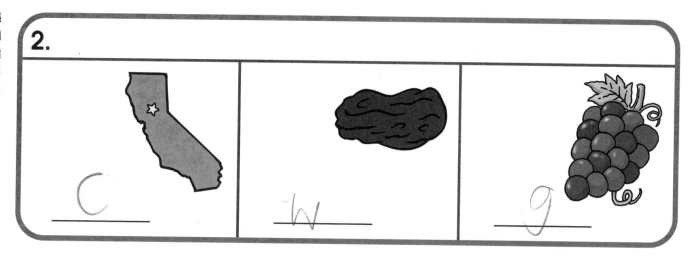

C _____   w _____   g _____

3.

nest	rock
dock	mother
brother	best
eight	date

Directions:

Ending Consonants (1): Ask students to say each picture aloud and listen to the ending sound. They then should write the ending letter on the line below the picture.

Blends (2): Ask students to say each picture aloud and listen to the beginning sound. They then should write the beginning blend on the line below the picture.

Rhyme Time (3): Have students draw lines connecting the words that rhyme.

Little Duckling?

The boy opens the barn doors. He holds a large pail. The boy smiles at Mama Duck and Little Duck.

What do you think is inside the pail?

"Hello, Mama Duck and Little Duckling," says the boy. The boy reaches into a pail full of bread crumbs.

What do you think the boy will do next?

"Little Duckling?" thought Little Duck. "I am not Little Duckling, I am Little Duck."

Why is Little Duck upset?

The boy holds out his hand. "Come here, Little Duckling. I have some tasty bread crumbs for you."

What should Little Duck do?

Name _____

Exceptional Endings and Blends

1.

g

B

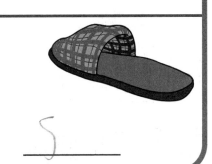
m

2.

f

shr

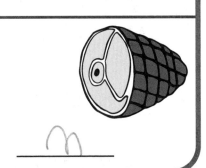
s

3. It is sharp.
It can hurt you.
Be careful when you use it.
What is it?

An eraser

A pair of scissors

A piece of paper

4. It is chewy.
You can blow bubbles with it.
What is it?

Ice cream

Gum

Soda

Directions:
Ending Consonants (1): Ask students to say each picture aloud and listen to the ending sound. They then should write the ending letter on the line below the picture.
Blends (2): Ask students to say each picture aloud and listen to the beginning sound. They then should write the beginning blend on the line below the picture.
Making Sense (3-4): Ask students to circle the answer that makes the most sense.

Quack, Quack, Quack

bad

Little Duck did not come closer. He was not "Little Duckling." He was Little Duck. And he would not eat bread crumbs if he was not called the right name.

How is Little Duck behaving?

yes

"What's the matter, Little Duckling?" asks the boy. The boy bends down and pats Little Duck's soft head.

Do you think Little Duck likes it when the boy pats his head?

mecus yes
sore

"Wow. You have gotten big," says the boy. "I will call you Little Duck from now on."

Why do you think the boy will call him Little Duck?"

hape

Little Duck quacks three times. Then, he eats bread crumbs from the boy's hand.

How does Little Duck feel now?

Endless Endings

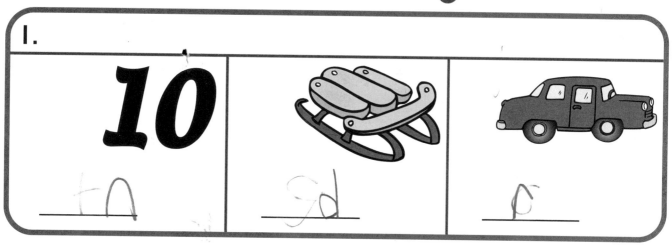

1.

10   _____   _____   _____

2. school   student   teacher   doctor

3. bird   frog   human   dog

4. circle   two   eight   six

5.

<u>There are four birds.</u>
There are five birds.

6.

There are 5-2 toads.
There are 1+3 toads.

Directions:

Ending Consonants (1): Ask students to say each picture aloud and listen to the ending sound. They then should write the ending letter on the line below the picture.

Classification (2-4): Have students look at all four pictures or words in each row and then circle the three that belong together.

Using the Pictures (5-6): Have students look at the pictures in each box. Then, have them circle the sentence that describes the picture.

Brrr!

Little Duck dips his foot into the pond. The water is so cold. "Brrr!" says Little Duck.

Have you ever felt cold water like Little Duck?

Yes

KDS.

Mama Duck laughs and says, "It is not cold, Little Duck. Plus, you're a duck. Our feathers keep us warm in cold water."

How do people keep warm when it is cold?

to eat him.

Little Duck wades into the water. The water is cold, but nice. Maybe Little Duck will see the fish again.

Why does Little Duck want to see fish again?

a shark.

Something strange is in the water. "Mama Duck, what is that?" asks Little Duck.

What do you think is in the water?

More Endings

1.

_____ A   _____ S   _____ t

2.

_____ e   _____ S   _____ A

3. Write a sentence that includes one of the words above in #2.

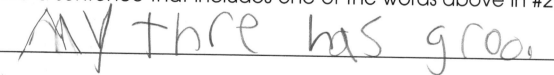

My thre has groo.

_____

Directions:

Ending Consonants (1): Ask students to say each picture aloud and listen to the ending sound. They then should write the ending letter on the line below the picture.

Blends (2): Ask students to say each picture aloud and listen to the beginning sound. They then should write the beginning blend on the line below the picture.

Writing Time (3): See directions in #3.

New Friend

Yes.

Little Duck and his mom swim closer to the strange thing. A girl duck comes up from the water.

Have you ever felt water like Little Duck?

fish.

"Wow, that was fun!" says the girl duck. "I love diving in the water."

Do you think she is looking for something? What?

"You don't think it is too cold?" asks Little Duck.

"No," she says. "The water is just right. My name is Matilda. What's yours?"

I doNt no

"My name is Little Duck."

What do you think happens next?

Keep on Blending

1.

f _____   K _____   y _____

2.

f _____   s _____   p _____

3.

3 _____   1 _____   2 _____

Directions:

Ending Consonants (1): Ask students to say each picture aloud and listen to the ending sound. They then should write the ending letter on the line below the picture.

Blends (2): Ask students to say each picture aloud and listen to the beginning sound. They then should write the beginning blend on the line below the picture.

Sequence (3): Have your students look at all three pictures. Ask the students to write **1** below the event that would happen first, **2** below the event that would happen second, and **3** below the event that would happen third.

Snails Away!

"Do you want to dive for snails, Little Duck?" asks Matilda. "They live at the bottom of the pond."

Do you think Little Duck will say yes or no? Why?

no

"I don't know how to dive," says Little Duck.

"Sure you do. All ducks know how to dive," says Matilda.

Do you think Little Duck will know how to dive?

no

"I'll try," says Little Duck and he dives into the water. It is fun underwater. But Little Duck doesn't see any snails.

What other things might Little Duck see underwater?

fish

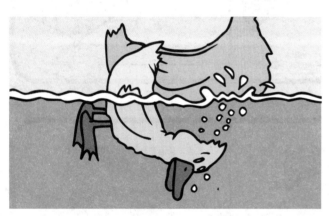

Little Duck and Matilda come up for air. They didn't catch even one snail. "Well," says Matilda, "there is only one thing to be done."

What do you think Little Duck and Matilda will do next?

go home

Is the End in Sight?

1.

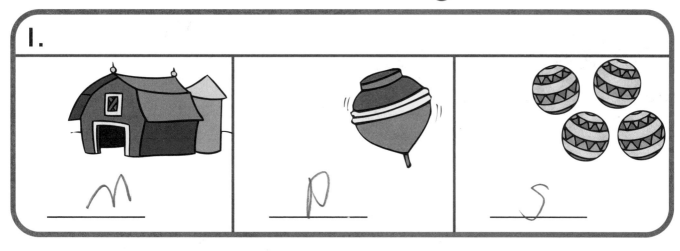

M _____   p _____   S _____

2.

t _____   St _____   g _____

3.

seven	brick
trick	eleven
sneak	leak
treat	beat

Directions:

Ending Consonants (1): Ask students to say each picture aloud and listen to the ending sound. They then should write the ending letter on the line below the picture.

Blends (2): Ask students to say each picture aloud and listen to the beginning sound. They then should write the beginning blend on the line below the picture.

Rhyme Time (3): Have students draw lines connecting the words that rhyme.

Little Duck and Matilda Go to the Farm

Little Duck and Matilda waddle along the side of the road. "Where are we going?" asks Little Duck.

Where do you think they are going?

"We are going to the farm on the hill. The farmer throws away old corn. He throws away stale bread. He throws away grass clippings," says Matilda.

Would you want to eat stale bread? Why or why not?

"What do we do now?" asks Little Duck.

"We will take some of this home with us," says Matilda.

"We are going to make some duck soup," says Matilda.

"Does duck soup taste good?" asks Little Duck.

"Duck soup tastes very good. You'll see," says Matilda.

Do you think duck soup will taste good?

Valuable Vowels

1.

cake   pond   piy

2.

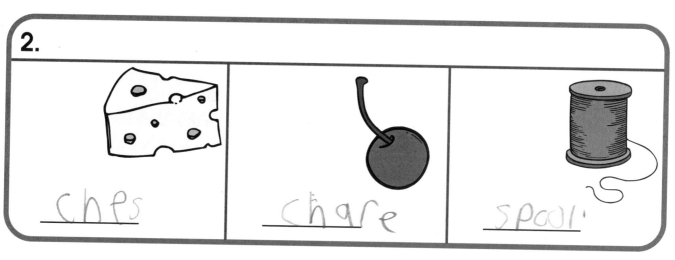

ches   chare   spool

3.

onedjmdii   onenickel

Directions:

Long Vowels (1): Have students name each picture. Then, your students should write the long vowel on the line provided.

Dynamite Digraphs (2): Review the **ch** digraph. Students should name each picture. They should write **ch** below each picture that begins with the **ch** sound.

One or More (3): Have your students look at all four pictures. Ask your student to identify the pictures with only one (singular) object. Your student should write down his or her answers.

Duck Soup

na

Matilda and Little Duck sit by the edge of the pond. "What is in duck soup?" asks Little Duck.

Would you want to eat duck soup?

corn

"Close your eyes and take a guess," says Matilda. "Duck soup is the best soup in the whole world."

What do you think Little Duck tastes?

gras.

"I taste corn," says Little Duck, "and I taste bread crumbs. And I taste something green."

What do you think Little Duck tastes that is green?

no

"Good guess, Little Duck," says Matilda. "Duck soup is made of corn, water, bread crumbs, and grass. Yummy for ducks."

Do you think you would like to eat a bowl of duck soup?

Name _____

Vowels

1.

o	o	i

2.

Sh	Sh	~~o~~

3.

one fork   one nit

Directions:

Long Vowels (1): Have students name each picture. Then, the students should write the long vowel on the line provided.

Dynamite Digraphs (2): Review the **sh** digraph. Students should name each picture. They should write **sh** below each picture that begins with the **sh** sound.

One or More (3): Have your student look at all four pictures. Ask your student to identify the pictures with only one (singular) object. Your student should write down his or her answers.

Little Duck Dives

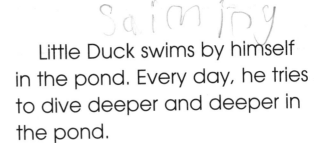

Little Duck swims by himself in the pond. Every day, he tries to dive deeper and deeper in the pond.

What do you like to practice?

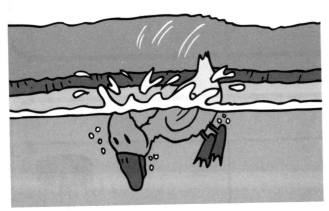

Little Duck wants to find a snail to give to Matilda. One day, he sees something at the bottom of the pond.

What do you think Little Duck sees?

Little Duck swims deeper and deeper to the pond bottom. Something is shiny. It is not a snail.

What do you think is at the bottom?

"What is this?" says Little Duck. He carries a penny in his beak and puts it in the grass.

What do you think Little Duck will do with the penny he found?

Name _____

Dynamite Digraphs

1.

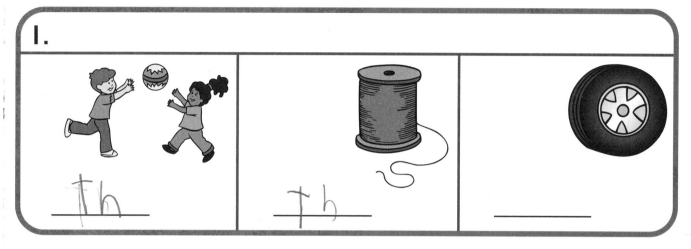

___Th___   ___Th___   _____

2.

___a___   ___e___   ___o___

3.

___thanks___   ___chips___

Directions:

Dynamite Digraphs (1): Review the **th** digraph. Students should name each picture. They should write **th** below each picture that begins with the **th** sound.

Long Vowels (2): Have students name each picture. Then, your students should write the long vowel on the line provided.

Double Time: Blends and Digraphs (3): Write two words that start with a blend and end with a consonant digraph. Example: French.

What to Do With a Penny

get food

"What should we do with the penny?" asks Little Duck. "Should we add it to the duck soup? Maybe it will taste good with the corn, bread crumbs, and grass?"

What do you think Matilda and Little Duck should do with the penny?

yes

"I don't think you can eat a penny," says Matilda. "Why don't we ask your mom if she knows what to do with it?"

What do you think Mama Duck will say?

BY STUP

Little Duck and Matilda waddle over to Mama Duck. "Mama Duck, what should we do with a penny?" asks Little Duck.

What are some things you would do with a penny?

yes

"Well, you should throw the penny back into the pond and make a wish," says Mama Duck.

Would you want to throw the penny back and make a wish?

Name _____

Dynamite Digraphs

I.

_wh_____   _____   _wh_____

2.

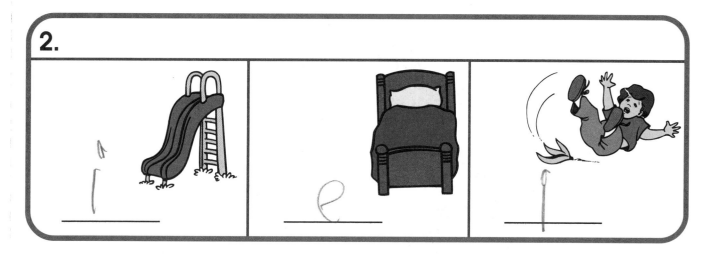

_i_____   _e_____   _i_____

3.

_3___ The crowd cheers.

_1___ The batter comes to the plate.

_2___ The batter strikes out.

Directions:

Dynamite Digraphs (1): Review the **wh** digraph. Students should name each picture. They should write **wh** below each picture that begins with the **wh** sound.

Vowels (2): Have students name each picture. Then, your students should write the vowel on the line provided.

Sequence (3): Have your students read all three sentences. Ask your students to write **1** next to the event that would happen first, **2** next to the event that would happen second, and **3** next to the event that would happen third.

Spectrum Reading Grade 1

35

Make a Wish, Little Duck

a pool

"What should I wish for?" asks Little Duck. "I already have everything I want. I have the best Mama Duck, and I have a best friend."

What would you wish for?

a dad

"Well, isn't there anything else you want, Little Duck?" asks Mama Duck.

What could Little Duck wish for?

yes

"I guess I wish I could fly like the big ducks in the sky," says Little Duck. He throws the penny back in the pond.

Do you think Little Duck makes a good wish?

a Brd

"But Little Duck, your wish has already come true. You can fly!" says Mama Duck and kisses him on the head.

What other animals can fly?

Beautiful Beginnings

1.

_____   _____   _____

2.   _i_tch_

3.   _t_ch_

4.   _sh_

5.   _wh_

6.   _ch_

7.   _ch_

Directions:

Vowels (1): Have students name each picture. Then, your students should write the vowel on the line provided.

Dynamite Digraphs (2-7): Students should name each picture. They should write the digraph or blend used in each word below each picture.

Little Duck Is Scared

yes

Little Duck stands at the edge of the pond. "I am scared, Mama Duck. What if I fall? I don't think I can fly," says Little Duck.

Will it be bad if Little Duck falls?

yes

"Little Duck, don't think so much," says Mama Duck. "Just count one, two, three. Then, spread your wings and flap them up and down. Soon, you will be flying."

Do you think Little Duck can fly?

no

Little Duck counts, "One, two, three." He flaps his wings and stops. "I just can't do this. I am not like the other ducks."

Do you think Little Duck is right?

"Come on, Little Duck," says Matilda. "We can try together." Matilda flaps her wings. "One, two, three!" Matilda is flying. Little Duck watches from the ground.

Go Short or Go Long: A a

1. ate _Long_
2. at _short_
3. ape _Long_
4. act _short_
5. ant _short_
6. age _Long_
7. rake _rake_
8. ray _ray_
9. able _Lg_
10. rat _short_
11. rack _Long_
12. rate _short_
13. Andy _Long_
14. Alex _short_
15. Abe _Long_

Directions:
Vowels (1-15): Have students say each word aloud. Then, your students should write **short** or **long** next to the word.

Little Duck Tries

yes

Little Duck looks up at Matilda. She is flying in the sky. "Come on, Little Duck. I know you can do it!" she calls.

Do you think Little Duck can fly?

Happe

"Just try, Little Duck," says Mama Duck. "Count one, two, three, and flap your wings. I know you can do it, too."

Are you ever afraid to try something new? How do you think Little Duck is feeling?

yes

Little Duck looks at his mom. Next, he looks at Matilda flying in the sky. "Okay. I will try," says Little Duck.

How are Mama Duck and Matilda helping Little Duck?

Happe

Little Duck starts to flap his wings. "One," he says and lifts his wings. "Two," he says, and lifts them again. "Threeeeeee!" Little Duck flies!

How do you think Little Duck feels about himself?

Go Short or Go Long: E e

1. pen _short_

2. pencil _short_

3. plea _L_

4. pea _Long_

5. glee _Long_

6. green _Long_

7. tea _Long_

8. ten _short_

9. teen _short_

10. hen _short_

11. fence _short_

12. bee _Long_

13. be _Long_

14. bend _short_

15. Ben _short_

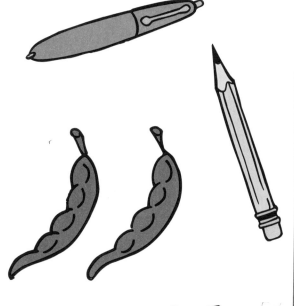

green

Directions:
Vowels (1-15): Have students say each word aloud. Then, your students should write **short** or **long** next to the word.

Little Duck and Matilda Fly

yes

Little Duck and Matilda are flying. "Wow! This is fun!" says Little Duck.

"I knew you would like it," says Matilda.

Do you think flying would be fun?

no

Little Duck flaps his wings harder. He moves higher in the sky. Next, he glides through the air. Little Duck moves his wings slower. Now, he moves closer to the ground.

Have you ever watched ducks fly?

some can see

"Wow! I think I get it! I think I know how to fly," says Little Duck.

"You are doing great!" says Matilda. "Just watch out for clouds."

"Why?" asks Little Duck.

Why should Little Duck watch out for clouds?

I dont no

Little Duck turns to look at Matilda. He does not see the cloud ahead. "Little Duck! Watch out!" calls Matilda. Little Duck flies right into a giant cloud.

What do you think will happen next?

Go Short or Go Long: I i

1. pie _____Long_____

2. pin _____sort_____

3. pine _____Long_____

4. pink _____sort_____

5. pit _____sart_____

6. tin _____sort_____

7. time _____time_____

8. tiny _____tiny_____

9. tick _____short_____

10. Tim _____short_____

11. die _____Long_____

12. dim _____dim_____

13. diet _____Long_____

14. dine _____dine_____

15. dinner _____diner_____

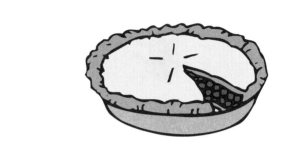

Directions:

Vowels (1-15): Have students say each word aloud. Then, your students should write **short** or **long** next to the word.

A Cloud

He is going

Little Duck flies into a cloud. He can't see anything. Everything is white and hazy. The air gets bumpy, too. "Oh, no!" calls Little Duck.

What is happening?

FliN

Little Duck starts to fall. He tumbles around and around. Little Duck is falling out of the cloud. He is falling through the sky. He is falling towards the hard ground.

What should Little Duck do?

H cant see

"Little Duck, flap your wings! Flap your wings hard," calls Matilda. Little Duck is so dizzy. He keeps falling and falling. Little Duck is close to the ground.

Why is Little Duck so dizzy?

Hes saf

"Little Duck, you must flap your wings!" calls Mama Duck. Little Duck sucks in air. He flaps one wing. He flaps the other. "Flap harder, Little Duck! Flap harder!" Little Duck flaps his wings as fast as he can.

What will happen to Little Duck?

Name _____

Go Short or Go Long: O o

1. pot _sort_

2. spot _sort_

3. snow _Long_

4. not _sort_

5. oat _Long_

6. on _sort_

7. box _sort_

8. mop _sort_

9. rope _Long_

10. Oliver _sort_

11. show _Long_

12. shop _sort_

13. clock _sort_

14. stop _sort_

15. slope _Long_

Directions:
Vowels (1-15): Have students say each word aloud. Then, your students should write **short** or **long** next to the word.

Spectrum Reading Grade 1

45

Little Duck Soars

Little Duck flaps his wings as hard as he can. He shoots up in the air again! "Good job, Little Duck! Good job!" calls Mama Duck from the ground.

How do you think Mama Duck feels?

Little Duck flaps his wings. Little Duck shakes his head. He calls to Mama Duck below, "It's okay, Mama Duck! It's okay!"

Matilda flies next to him. "Oh my, Little Duck! You scared me. Are you all right?" she asks.

Little Duck smiles. "Yup. I'll try never to fly into a cloud again. But I can really fly, Matilda! I can do it!"

How is Little Duck feeling?

Little Duck is so happy. He flaps his wings hard. He shoots higher and higher in the sky. "Yea!" he shouts. "Honk, Honk!" he calls. Matilda and Mama Duck watch him soar.

What has changed about Little Duck?

Go Short or Go Long: U u

1. under _____

2. cube _____

3. umbrella _____

4. cut _____

5. cute _____

6. butter _____

7. yummy _____

8. mule _____

9. club _____

10. duck _____

11. dune _____

12. tuck _____

13. tune _____

14. run _____

15. funny _____

Directions:
Vowels (1-15): Have students say each word aloud. Then, your students should write **short** or **long** next to the word.

Name _____

Big Time Rhyme

1. funny

2. honey

3. duck

4. stop

5. ton

6. snow

7. bear

8. spring

9. fall

10. tell

11. tear

Directions:
Rhyme Time (1-11): Have students draw lines connecting the words to the pictures that rhyme.

Classified Information

1.	sad	glad	mad	cage
2.	five	alive	nine	thirteen
3.	boat	don't	won't	did
4.	wheat	seat	beat	cat
5.	pie	pine	pin	spine
6.	jump	true	cube	June
7.	oat	coat	spot	moat
8.	glee	green	gem	greet
9.	hen	ten	tent	teen
10.	ray	rat	rake	rate

Directions:
Grouping Together (1-10): Have students read all four words in each line. Have students circle the three words that share the same vowel sound.

Carolyn Dreams of a Pet

Carolyn looked around her room. There were animals everywhere. She had teddy bears from her grandma. She had stuffed animals from her aunt. She even had posters of puppies on the wall. But what Carolyn wanted was a real pet. She wanted a kitten or a puppy to love and play with.

What do you dream of? Do you have a pet? Would you want one?

Name _____

Reading Skills

1. This story is about

   _____ Carolyn wanting a pet.

   _____ Carolyn wanting a toy.

   _____ how Carolyn is sad.

2. Carolyn has posters on the walls of

   _____ horses. _____ puppies. _____ flowers.

Word Play

1. What is a word that rhymes with *kitten*? _____

2. What is the beginning blend in this word? plane _____

3. What letter is missing from this word? g_____rl

Thinking Further and Predicting Outcomes

1. Do you think Carolyn will get a real pet or more teddy bears?

Directions:
Reading Skills Finding the main idea **(1):** Have students read the question and mark the correct answer. Story Details or Cause and Effect **(2):** Have students read the question and mark the correct answer.
Word Play (1-3): Have students read each question carefully and then write their answer or answers on the lines provided. Word play questions will include the following: rhyming words; identifying blends, digraphs, and missing letters; picture clues; and using the correct word.
Thinking Further and Predicting Outcomes (1): Have students read each question and then on a separate piece of paper write down and/or discuss their thoughts, opinions, and predictions. As the stories progress, have students discuss whether their predictions were accurate.

Carolyn Talks to Her Mom

Carolyn's mom was reading a book in the den. "Mom, can I ask you something?" asked Carolyn.

"Sure, Honey," said Mrs. Jones.

"Mom, I know I have teddy bears from Grandma. I even have stuffed animals from Aunt Linda. But I really want a pet I can hold and take care of," said Carolyn.

Carolyn's mom put down her book. "Pets take a lot of work," said Mrs. Jones. "And you don't just take care of a pet for a day, or a week, or even a month. Pets are part of the family for years. Do you think you would have time to take care of a pet? Why don't you really think about it."

Do you have a pet? Do you think pets are hard to take care of?

Name _____

Reading Skills

1. This story is about

_____Carolyn hearing about how pets are bad.

_____Carolyn hearing about how pets take work.

_____Carolyn hearing about how dirty pets are.

2. Carolyn's aunt's name is _____Lucinda. _____Lucy. _____Linda.

Word Play

1. What is a word that rhymes with *money*? _____

2. What is the beginning blend in this word? proud _____

3. What letter is missing from this word? A_____nt Linda

Thinking Further and Predicting Outcomes

1. Do you think Carolyn would take good care of a pet?

2. Do you think Carolyn's mother will help her buy a pet?

Directions:
Reading Skills Finding the main idea **(1):** Have students read the question and mark the correct answer. Story Details or Cause and Effect **(2):** Have students read the question and mark the correct answer.
Word Play (1-3): Have students read each question carefully and then write their answer or answers on the lines provided. Word play questions will include the following: rhyming words; identifying blends, digraphs, and missing letters; picture clues; and using the correct word.
Thinking Further and Predicting Outcomes (1-2): Have students read each question and then on a separate piece of paper write down and/or discuss their thoughts, opinions, and predictions. As the stories progress, have students discuss whether their predictions were accurate.

Time for a Pet

Carolyn went back to her room. She had just started school. Her new teacher gave her lots of homework. She had books to read and stories to write. Her class was even going to put on a school play.

Maybe she didn't have time to take care of a pet after all. Carolyn held her teddy bear tight. "What do you think I should do, teddy bear?" she asked. But the teddy bear didn't say anything at all because he wasn't real.

Do you think Carolyn has time to take care of a pet? Why or why not?

Reading Skills

I. In this story,

_____Carolyn thinks that she will have lots of time to care for a pet.

_____Carolyn thinks she might not have enough time for a pet.

_____Carolyn decides she doesn't want a pet.

2. Carolyn talks to her _____Aunt. _____teddy bear. _____posters.

Word Play

I. What is a word that rhymes with *bear*? _____

2. What is the beginning blend in this word? trade _____

3. What letter is missing from this word? Teddy b_____ar

Thinking Further and Predicting Outcomes

I. Do you think Carolyn can handle both a pet and school work?

2. Do you think if Carolyn gets a pet she will take good care of it?

Directions:
Reading Skills Finding the main idea **(1):** Have students read the question and mark the correct answer. Story Details or Cause and Effect **(2):** Have students read the question and mark the correct answer.
Word Play (1-3): Have students read each question carefully and then write their answer or answers on the lines provided. Word play questions will include the following: rhyming words; identifying blends, digraphs, and missing letters; picture clues; and using the correct word.
Thinking Further and Predicting Outcomes (1-2): Have students read each question and then on a separate piece of paper write down and/or discuss their thoughts, opinions, and predictions. As the stories progress, have students discuss whether their predictions were accurate.

Knock, Knock

"Knock, knock," said Carolyn's dad. He stood in the doorway. "Hi, Carolyn. Mom said you wanted a pet. What kind of pet did you want?"

"Hi, Dad. I want a pet that is soft like a kitten or a puppy," said Carolyn.

"Well, pets like dogs and cats are a lot of work," said Mr. Jones. "How about a pet turtle or a fish tank with lots of pretty fish? We could get a blue fish or maybe even an orange-and-white clown fish. What do you say?"

But Carolyn was sad. She knew she could never hug a turtle or a fish.

What is your favorite animal? Do some animals make better pets than others?

Name _____

Reading Skills

1. In this story,

   _____Carolyn's dad tells her she can't have a pet.

   _____Carolyn's dad talks about other types of pets.

   _____Carolyn's dad says he will buy her a dog.

2. Carolyn's dad mentions a possible pet. It is a

   _____turtle. _____bunny. _____pony.

Word Play

1. What are two words that rhyme with *fish*? _____

2. What is the beginning blend in this word? from _____

3. What letter is missing from this word? clo_____n fish

Thinking Further and Predicting Outcomes

1. Do you think Carolyn would enjoy a pet turtle?

Directions:

Reading Skills Finding the main idea (1): Have students read the question and mark the correct answer. Story Details or Cause and Effect (2): Have students read the question and mark the correct answer.

Word Play (1-3): Have students read each question carefully and then write their answer or answers on the lines provided. Word play questions will include the following: rhyming words; identifying blends, digraphs, and missing letters; picture clues; and using the correct word.

Thinking Further and Predicting Outcomes (1): Have students read each question and then on a separate piece of paper write down and/or discuss their thoughts, opinions, and predictions. As the stories progress, have students discuss whether their predictions were accurate.

I Promise

Carolyn sat down for breakfast with her mom and dad. She filled her bowl with cereal. "Mom and Dad," said Carolyn, "I know I can take care of a pet. I will help feed it every morning. I will fill its bowl with water. I promise, I will always take care of it. We can name our pet 'Promise.'"

Carolyn's mom and dad looked at each other. Carolyn's mom said, "Wow, you make a good case for a pet. Dad and I will have a long talk. We will tell you our answer tomorrow."

What do you think Carolyn's parents will say? Explain your answer.

Reading Skills

1. In this story,

_____ Carolyn explains how she would take care of her new pet.

_____ Carolyn says she is sad.

_____ Carolyn talks about her friends at school.

2. The pet will be named _____ Prince. _____ Promise. _____ Misty.

Word Play

1. What is the short vowel sound in *help*? _____

2. What is the ending consonant in this word? father _____

3. What letter is missing from this word? Promi_____e

Thinking Further and Predicting Outcomes

1. Do you think Carolyn has explained herself well?

2. Do you think her parents like Carolyn's plan?

Directions:
Reading Skills Finding the main idea (1): Have students read the question and mark the correct answer. Story Details or Cause and Effect (2): Have students read the question and mark the correct answer.
Word Play (1-3): Have students read each question carefully and then write their answer or answers on the lines provided. Word play questions will include the following: rhyming words; identifying blends, diagraphs, and missing letters; picture clues; and using the correct word.
Thinking Further and Predicting Outcomes (1-2): Have students read each question and then on a separate piece of paper write down and/or discuss their thoughts, opinions, and predictions. As the stories progress, have students discuss whether their predictions were accurate.

Yes or No?

All night, Carolyn tossed in her bed. She knew she could take care of a pet. She hoped her parents would say *yes*. She would give her pet fresh water. She would brush its fur. And she would always love it.

Carolyn's last name was Jones. So her new pet would be named "Promise Jones." She liked the name already.

Carolyn ran down the stairs at 7:00 in the morning. "Wow, you are up early!" said Carolyn's mom.

"Can we get Promise?" asked Carolyn.

"Let's call your dad in the kitchen and see," said Carolyn's mom.

Why do you think Carolyn tossed in her bed all night? Why did she get up so early?

Name _____

Reading Skills

1. This story is about

_____Carolyn waking up early to find out if she will get a pet.

_____Carolyn waking up early to go to school.

_____Carolyn sleeping because she is so tired.

2. Carolyn's last name is _____Jones. _____Promise. _____Linda.

Word Play

1. Which is the correct word for this sentence?

You _____ have a pet.
can't kant cent

2. What is the long vowel in this word? snow _____

3. What letter is missing from this word? Carolyn J_____nes

Thinking Further and Predicting Outcomes

1. What will the decision be?

2. Why do people love pets?

Directions:
Reading Skills Finding the main idea **(1):** Have students read the question and mark the correct answer. Story Details or Cause and Effect **(2):** Have students read the question and mark the correct answer.
Word Play (1-3): Have students read each question carefully and then write their answer or answers on the lines provided. Word play questions will include the following: rhyming words; identifying blends, digraphs, and missing letters; picture clues; and using the correct word.
Thinking Further and Predicting Outcomes (1-2): Have students read each question and then on a separate piece of paper write down and/or discuss their thoughts, opinions, and predictions. As the stories progress, have students discuss whether their predictions were accurate.

A Real Pet

Carolyn's dad walked into the kitchen. He had a big smile on his face. Carolyn was jumping in her seat. Her dad smiled like that when he said something good.

"Carolyn, your mom and I have talked all night about a pet," said her dad. "Now, if you promise to take good care of a pet, we will get one."

Carolyn ran to her dad and hugged him. Carolyn's mom joined the hug. The Jones family would soon have a real pet.

Why do you think Carolyn's parents said *yes*? Do you think Carolyn will keep her promise?

Name _____

Reading Skills

1. This story is about

    _____Carolyn finding out that she will get a pet.

    _____Carolyn finding out that she will not get a pet.

    _____Carolyn finding out she's late for school.

2. Carolyn hugged her _____mother. _____father. _____parents.

Word Play

1. What's a word that rhymes with *dog*? _____

2. What is the beginning sound (digraph) in this word?
   child _____

3. Which letters are missing from this sentence?
   Carolyn will have a pet for _____self.
   her it him

Thinking Further and Predicting Outcomes

1. Where will the Jones family get their pet?

2. Do you think Carolyn's parents made the right decision?

Directions:

Reading Skills Finding the main idea **(1):** Have students read the question and mark the correct answer. Story Details or Cause and Effect **(2):** Have students read the question and mark the correct answer.

Word Play (1-3): Have students read each question carefully and then write their answer or answers on the lines provided. Word play questions will include the following: rhyming words; identifying blends, digraphs, and missing letters; picture clues; and using the correct word.

Thinking Further and Predicting Outcomes (1-2): Have students read each question and then on a separate piece of paper write down and/or discuss their thoughts, opinions, and predictions. As the stories progress, have students discuss whether their predictions were accurate.

Today a Pet

"Carolyn, after school we will go to the pound. There, we will look for a pet that needs a home," said Mrs. Jones.

Carolyn was so excited in school. "I'm going to get a pet today!" Carolyn told her friends.

"What kind of pet are you going to get?" asked her friend Freddy. "Will you get an alligator?"

"Nope," said Carolyn.

"Will you get a goldfish?" asked Freddy.

"Nope," said Carolyn.

"I hope to get a kitten or a puppy," said Carolyn.

Would an alligator make a good pet? Would a goldfish make a good pet? Why or why not?

Name _____

Reading Skills

1. This story is about

   _____Carolyn telling her friends about getting a pet.

   _____Carolyn telling her friends about her
   school project.

   _____Carolyn's visit to the pound.

2. What was the name of Carolyn's friend who asked about her new
   pet? His name is _____Freddy. _____Eddie. _____Betty.

Word Play

1. What is a word that rhymes with *pound*? _____

2. What is the beginning sound (digraph) in this word? think _____

3. Which word is missing from this sentence?
   Carolyn will go to the pound _____ her mom.
   with   near   by

Thinking Further and Predicting Outcomes

1. Do you think Carolyn will show her pet to her classmates?

Directions:
Reading Skills Finding the main idea (1): Have students read the question and mark the correct answer. Story Details or Cause and Effect
(2): Have students read the question and mark the correct answer.
Word Play (1-3): Have students read each question carefully and then write their answer or answers on the lines provided. Word play questions
will include the following: rhyming words; identifying blends, digraphs, and missing letters; picture clues; and using the correct word.
Thinking Further and Predicting Outcomes (1): Have students read each question and then on a separate piece of paper write down and/or
discuss their thoughts, opinions, and predictions. As the stories progress, have students discuss whether their predictions were accurate.

Two Good Things

"Mom, why are we going to the pound? Shouldn't we go to the pet store?" said Carolyn.

"The pound is an animal shelter. It is a place where lost or unwanted animals are brought," said Mrs. Jones. "These animals really need homes. If we can find an animal here, two good things happen. We get a family pet and an animal gets a home. The pound has all types of animals. We will see cats, dogs, and even some rabbits."

What would you do if you found a lost animal? Who would you tell?

Name _____

Reading Skills

1. This story is about

   _____Carolyn learning about the pound.

   _____Carolyn wanting to go to the pet store.

   _____Carolyn changing her mind about getting a pet.

2. Mrs. Jones and Carolyn will go to the

   _____pound. _____pet store. _____zoo.

Word Play

1. What is the plural of *store*? _____

2. What is the beginning sound (digraph) in this word?
   which _____

3. Which word is missing from this sentence?
   Carolyn _____ be upset today.
   won't don't she'll

Thinking Further and Predicting Outcomes

1. Do you think it's a good idea to go to the pound for a pet?

2. What will Carolyn do when she chooses her pet?

Directions:
Reading Skills Finding the main idea (1): Have students read the question and mark the correct answer. Story Details or Cause and Effect (2): Have students read the question and mark the correct answer.
Word Play (1-3): Have students read each question carefully and then write their answer or answers on the lines provided. Word play questions will include the following: rhyming words; identifying blends, digraphs, and missing letters; picture clues; and using the correct word.
Thinking Further and Predicting Outcomes (1-2): Have students read each question and then on a separate piece of paper write down and/or discuss their thoughts, opinions, and predictions. As the stories progress, have students discuss whether their predictions were accurate.

The Pound

Carolyn and her mom walked into a large room filled with rows of cages. Behind the bars were animals of all shapes and sizes. There were fat dogs, skinny dogs like hot dogs, furry dogs, and cages of cats. Carolyn reached her hand through the bars. She petted a sleeping kitten. Its tummy was moving up and down. Next, a fat cat licked Carolyn's hand. Its tongue felt scratchy on her hand.

What animal do you think Carolyn will pick? Why?

Name _____

Reading Skills

1. This story is about

   _____Carolyn seeing all sorts of animals at the pound.

   _____Carolyn feeling scared.

   _____Carolyn playing with a lizard.

2. Carolyn plays with a kitten that is
   _____eating. _____sleeping. _____drinking.

Word Play

1. What do the words *fat, skinny, thin,* and *large* have in common?

   _____

2. What is the beginning sound (digraph) in this word? throw _____

3. What letters are missing from this sentence?
   Carolyn plays with a ki_____en.

Thinking Further and Predicting Outcomes

1. Will Carolyn choose a pet after all?

2. Will Carolyn get more than one pet?

Directions:
Reading Skills Finding the main idea (1): Have students read the question and mark the correct answer. Story Details or Cause and Effect
(2): Have students read the question and mark the correct answer.
Word Play (1-3): Have students read each question carefully and then write their answer or answers on the lines provided. Word play questions
will include the following: rhyming words; identifying blends, digraphs, and missing letters; picture clues; and using the correct word.
Thinking Further and Predicting Outcomes (1-2): Have students read each question and then on a separate piece of paper write down and/or
discuss their thoughts, opinions, and predictions. As the stories progress, have students discuss whether their predictions were accurate.

Carolyn Is Sad

"Mom, who feeds all these animals?"

"The workers here feed them, but there are not enough people to brush them, or even love them."

"Mom, this makes me sad," said Carolyn.

"I know Carolyn, but we can only take one pet. And saving one animal is a good thing," said Mrs. Jones.

"Yes," said Carolyn, and she kept looking at all the cages.

Why does Carolyn feel sad? What does Mrs. Jones say that makes Carolyn feel better?

Reading Skills

1. This story is about

_____Carolyn realizing that taking care of only one pet is still a good thing.

_____Carolyn realizing that she should take five pets.

_____Carolyn leaving the pound with no pets.

2. The pets are living in _____cages. _____houses. _____boxes.

Word Play

1. What is the long vowel sound in *Jones*? _____

2. What is the ending consonant in this word? cages _____

3. What letter is missing from this word? po_____nd

Thinking Further and Predicting Outcomes

1. Do you think Carolyn will feel better about taking only one pet?

2. Do you think Carolyn is a caring person?

Directions:
Reading Skills Finding the main idea (1): Have students read the question and mark the correct answer. Story Details or Cause and Effect (2): Have students read the question and mark the correct answer.
Word Play (1-3): Have students read each question carefully and then write their answer or answers on the lines provided. Word play questions will include the following: rhyming words; identifying blends, digraphs, and missing letters; picture clues; and using the correct word.
Thinking Further and Predicting Outcomes (1-2): Have students read each question and then on a separate piece of paper write down and/or discuss their thoughts, opinions, and predictions. As the stories progress, have students discuss whether their predictions were accurate.

Promise Jones

Carolyn did not know what to do. So many animals needed a home and she could take only one. Carolyn went back to the sleeping kitten. It looked like a baby cloud. It was a tiny ball of soft fur. She reached her hand in the cage and petted it slowly. "I think I will take you," she said. "Your name will be Promise Jones." Just then, the kitten looked up at Carolyn.

Why do you think Carolyn chooses the kitten? What animal would you have picked? Do you think Carolyn picked a good name for her new pet? Why or why not?

Reading Skills

1. This story is about

   _____Carolyn choosing a kitten.

   _____Carolyn choosing a puppy.

   _____Carolyn choosing two puppies.

2. What color is the kitten that Carolyn chose?

   _____white.   _____black.   _____brown.

Word Play

1. What is the first short vowel sound in *kitten*? _____

2. What is *dad* spelled backwards? _____

3. Carolyn _____ a kitten.
   choose   chose   choiced

Thinking Further and Predicting Outcomes

1. Do you think Carolyn will always take good care of her kitten?

2. Do you think Carolyn will be happy with her new pet?

Directions:
Reading Skills Finding the main idea **(1):** Have students read the question and mark the correct answer. Story Details or Cause and Effect
(2): Have students read the question and mark the correct answer.
Word Play (1-3): Have students read each question carefully and then write their answer or answers on the lines provided. Word play questions
will include the following: rhyming words; identifying blends, digraphs, and missing letters; picture clues; and using the correct word.
Thinking Further and Predicting Outcomes (1-2): Have students read each question and then on a separate piece of paper write down and/or
discuss their thoughts, opinions, and predictions. As the stories progress, have students discuss whether their predictions were accurate.

A New Kitten

"Mom, I think this is our new pet," said Carolyn.

Carolyn's mom bent down and looked into the kitten's cage.

"Yes, a beautiful little kitten. I think she will like being part of our family. Let's tell the man at the desk that we have found our new pet," said Mrs. Jones.

The man behind the desk said, "New kittens need shots before they can go home with you. You can pick up your boy kitten tomorrow. He will need cat food, water, and a soft place to sleep."

Why do pets need shots? What else might a new kitten like to have?

Name _____

Reading Skills

1. In this story,

_____Carolyn realizes she cannot have her kitten until tomorrow.

_____Carolyn learns that the kitten belongs to someone.

_____Carolyn learns that the kitten is 3 years old.

2. The kitten is a _____boy. _____girl.

Word Play

1. What is the short vowel sound in *shot*?_____

2. What is the ending consonant in this word? shot _____

3. What letter is missing from this word? cat fo_____d

Thinking Further and Predicting Outcomes

1. Do you think Carolyn will be upset she can't have the kitten right away?

2. Do you think Carolyn will be nervous for the kitten because he needs a shot?

Directions:
Reading Skills Finding the main idea (1): Have students read the question and mark the correct answer. Story Details or Cause and Effect (2): Have students read the question and mark the correct answer.
Word Play (1-3): Have students read each question carefully and then write their answer or answers on the lines provided. Word play questions will include the following: rhyming words; identifying blends, digraphs, and missing letters; picture clues; and using the correct word.
Thinking Further and Predicting Outcomes (1-2): Have students read each question and then on a separate piece of paper write down and/or discuss their thoughts, opinions, and predictions. As the stories progress, have students discuss whether their predictions were accurate.

A Gift

Carolyn's dad was waiting at the front door of the house. He had a gift in his hand. Carolyn ran to her dad. "Dad, our new kitten comes tomorrow! He is so soft! He looks just like a cotton ball or a cloud," said Carolyn.

"Should we still call him Promise? If he is so soft, maybe we should call him Cloudy or Mr. Cotton," said Carolyn's dad.

"No. I already told him his name was Promise Jones," said Carolyn.

"Well, I bought food, litter, a litter box, and a gift for Promise Jones," said Carolyn's dad.

Carolyn unwrapped the gift. It was a soft cat bed shaped in a circle. A kitten would feel safe and warm inside it. Carolyn hugged her dad. "Promise Jones will love his new bed," she said.

What is the most important thing a new pet would need?

Reading Skills

1. This story is about

_____Carolyn getting a gift from her dad.

_____Carolyn learning to study.

_____Carolyn playing with Promise.

2. The new kitten is like a _____cotton ball. _____paper. _____snow.

Word Play

1. What word rhymes with *white*?_____

2. What is the ending consonant in this word? cotton _____

3. What letter is missing from this word? cott_____n

Thinking Further and Predicting Outcomes

1. Do you think Carolyn makes the right decision about keeping Promise's name the same?

2. Do you like soft things? Why?

Directions:
Reading Skills Finding the main idea **(1):** Have students read the question and mark the correct answer. Story Details or Cause and Effect
(2): Have students read the question and mark the correct answer.
Word Play (1-3): Have students read each question carefully and then write their answer or answers on the lines provided. Word play questions
will include the following: rhyming words; identifying blends, digraphs, and missing letters; picture clues; and using the correct word.
Thinking Further and Predicting Outcomes (1-2): Have students read each question and then on a separate piece of paper write down and/or
discuss their thoughts, opinions, and predictions. As the stories progress, have students discuss whether their predictions were accurate.

Promise Jones Comes Home

The next day, Promise Jones came home. Carolyn and her mom and dad sat in the family room. Slowly, they opened the kitten carrier.

First, one tiny, white foot pressed on the rug. Then, another tiny foot came out. Next came Promise Jones' head poking out of the carrier. "Hi, Promise Jones," said Carolyn. She held out her hand. Promise looked around the room.

"Meow," he said. He walked over to Carolyn. Carolyn held him in her arms. Then, she kissed his tiny head. Carolyn said, "Promise Jones, you have found a home. We promise."

Do you think Carolyn and her family will be happy with their new pet? Why or why not? Do you think Carolyn will keep her promise with her new kitten?

Name _____

Reading Skills

I. This story is about

_____Carolyn promising to care for her cat.

_____Carolyn eating dinner with her cat.

_____Carolyn having a party with her parents.

2. Carolyn plays with her new pet in the

_____bedroom. _____family room. _____kitchen.

Word Play

I. What words rhyme with *glad*? _____

2. What is the ending consonant in this word? plays _____

3. Carolyn will always _____ her kitten.
   love   like   tickle

Thinking Further and Predicting Outcomes

I. Do you think Carolyn will ever want another pet?

2. Would you want somebody like Carolyn as your friend?

Directions:
Reading Skills Finding the main idea (1): Have students read the question and mark the correct answer. Story Details or Cause and Effect
(2): Have students read the question and mark the correct answer.
Word Play (1-3): Have students read each question carefully and then write their answer or answers on the lines provided. Word play questions
will include the following: rhyming words; identifying blends, digraphs, and missing letters; picture clues; and using the correct word.
Thinking Further and Predicting Outcomes (1-2): Have students read each question and then on a separate piece of paper write down and/or
discuss their thoughts, opinions, and predictions. As the stories progress, have students discuss whether their predictions were accurate.

Name _____

Revisiting Blends

1.

 _____  _____  _____

2.

 _____  _____  _____

3. It has lots of animals.
It is fun to visit.
You can learn a lot.
What is it?

A school

a zoo

the moon

4. You can swim here.
It feels cool. Have fun!
What is it?

A pool

a bathtub

a glass of water

Directions:
Blends (1-2): Ask students to say each picture aloud and listen to the beginning sound. They then should write the beginning blend on the line below the picture.
Making Sense (3-4): Ask students to circle the answer that makes the most sense.

Finding the Correct Word

1. Do you like to _____ songs?

sing

sings

sang

2. The duck enjoys _____ corn.

eaten

eating

to eat

3. Jimmy has _____ into the pool.

jumping

jumped

jump

4. Josefina _____ to play piano.

like

likes

liking

5.

 _____

 _____

 _____

 _____

 _____

 _____

Directions:

Sentence Completion (1-4): Have students circle the word that best completes the sentence.

Sequence (5): Have the student look at all six pictures. Ask your student to write **1** below the event that would happen first, **2** below the event that would happen second, and so on.

Name _____

Blends Review

1.

_____   _____

2.

_____   _____

3.

_____   _____

4.

_____   _____

5.

_____   _____

6.

_____   _____

7.

_____   _____

8.

_____   _____

Directions:

Blends and Ending Consonants (1-8): Have your student look at each picture and say it aloud. Have your student listen to the beginning blends and ending consonants. Then, have your student write down the beginning blends and ending consonants next to each word.

Blends Review

1.

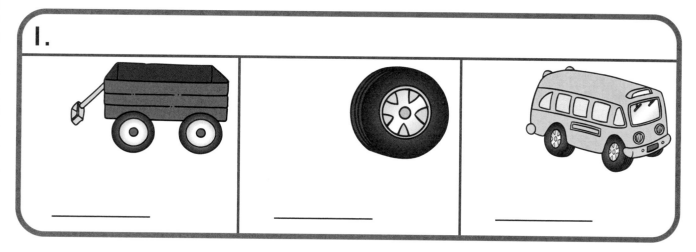

_____   _____   _____

2.

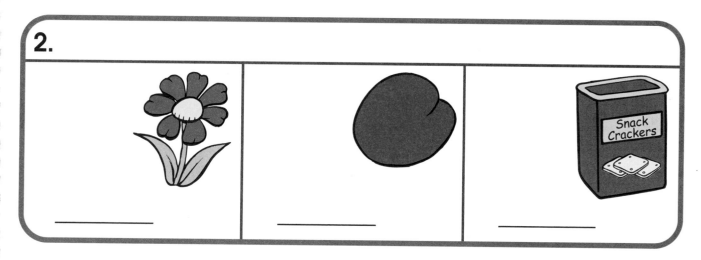

_____   _____   _____

3.

zba ___ ___ ___   hia ___ ___ ___

guk ___ ___ ___   bnu ___ ___ ___

Directions:

Beginning Consonants (1): Ask students to say each picture aloud and listen to the beginning sound. They then should write the beginning letter on the line below the picture.

Blends (2): Ask students to say each picture aloud and listen to the beginning sound. They then should write the beginning blend on the line below the picture.

Alphabetical Order (3): Ask students to put the three letters in each group in alphabetical order.

Where Are You?

1.

next to   over   above   below   in   over   under   below

2.

under   inside   around   below   outside   inside   under   below

3.

in   next to   around   above   in   beneath   under   next to

4.

down   up   sideways   under   down   up   around   near

Directions:

Using the Pictures (1-4): Have your student look at the pictures. Ask your student to circle the word that describes where the objects are located.

Classify Me

1.	three	six	five	food
2.	orange	lemon	lime	ham
3.	penny	dime	nickel	dollar
4.	mouse	rat	bug	lion
5.	truck	car	boat	bus
6.	June	July	August	flag
7.	green	yellow	brown	tired
8.	stone	rock	brick	rug
9.	mom	dad	dog	sister
10.	funny	smile	laugh	mad

Directions:

Grouping Together (1-10): Have students read all four words in each line. Have students circle the three words that go together.

Alaska

Alaska is the largest state in America. It is the coldest state. It is two times as big as Texas and home to bears and eagles. If you lived in Alaska you might see a blue glacier shining in the sun. Maybe you would see a bear, a moose, or even a pod of whales.

Juneau is the capital of Alaska, named after Joe Juneau. He went to Alaska in search of gold.

Many people in Alaska like to make and eat special ice cream. They mix berries with snow and seal oil.

Reading Skills

1. What might you see if you lived in Alaska?

_____robins

_____moose

_____lions

2. Alaska is _____ as big as Texas.
   two times three times ten times

3. What did Joe Juneau search for in Alaska? _____
   bears gold diamonds

Word Play

1. Write one other word that you can make from the word *Alaska*. _____

2. Write one other word that rhymes with *bear*. _____

3. If you _____ in Alaska, you should own a hat.
   live liked

Thinking Further

1. Would you want to live in Alaska? Why or why not?

2. What are a few words that describe Alaska?

Directions:
Reading Skills–Comprehension and Facts and Details (1-3): Have students read the question and mark the correct answer.
Word Play (1-3): Have students read each question carefully and then write their answer or answers on the lines provided. Word play questions will include the following: rhyming words, missing letters, finding words, picture clues, and using the correct word.
Thinking Further (1-2): Have students read each question and then discuss their responses, or have them write down their thoughts on a separate sheet of paper.

New Mexico

New Mexico is a state full of red clay mountains. The capital of New Mexico is Santa Fe. It is the oldest capital city in America. This very old city was founded in 1610!

In Taos, New Mexico, you can see brown adobe houses (made from clay bricks baked in the sun).

In New Mexico, you might see bunches of red chili peppers. These are hung on strings outside houses. Sometimes, people leave the red chilies out all winter. They look beautiful in the white snow.

SANTA FE

Name _____

Reading Skills

1. What might you see if you lived in New Mexico?

_____bunches of chili peppers

_____bunches of bananas

_____bunches of green peppers

2. Santa Fe was founded in _____1610. _____1615. _____1910.

Word Play

1. Write one other word that you can make from the word
New Mexico. _____

2. Write one other word that rhymes with
clay. _____

3. You can see _____ adobe homes in Taos.
  brown black

Thinking Further

1. Would you want to live in New Mexico? Why or why not?

2. What are a few words that describe New Mexico?

Oregon

Long, long ago many people heard secrets about Oregon. They headed where the soil was good for farming. Many people wanted to travel across America to this state. They wanted to plant crops.

Traveling across America in a covered wagon was very dangerous. Travelers could go only in summer. They had to beat the coming cold weather. Many people on the Oregon Trail did not have enough food or fresh water. Many travelers died.

Today, you can visit Oregon by car, plane, or train. Maybe you'd want to visit Crater Lake National Park and see America's deepest lake.

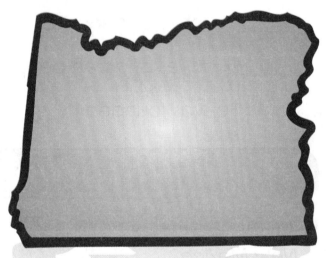

Name _____

Reading Skills

I. What might you see if you visited Oregon?

_____the deepest lake

_____the widest lake

_____the coldest lake

2. Some people went to Oregon because it had _____ soil.

               rich poor dirty

Word Play

I. Write one other word that you can make from the word
Oregon. _____

2. Write one other word that rhymes with
soil. _____

3. Oregon is _____ in the winter.
         cool cold

Thinking Further

I. Do you think there are farmers in Oregon? How do you know?

2. What are a few words that describe Oregon?

Directions:
Reading Skills–Comprehension and Facts and Details (1-2): Have students read the question and mark the correct answer.
Word Play (1-3): Have students read each question carefully and then write their answer or answers on the lines provided. Word play questions
will include the following: rhyming words, missing letters, finding words, picture clues, and using the correct word.
Thinking Further (1-2): Have students read each question and then discuss their responses, or have them write down their thoughts on a
separate sheet of paper.

Rhode Island

Rhode Island is the smallest state in America. It is nicknamed "Little Rhody."

If you visit, you might want to ride America's oldest merry-go-round in Watch Hill.

Maybe you'd want to take a ferry ride to Block Island. This is a tiny island off the coast. French pirates are said to have landed there. Captain Kidd's gold is thought to still be buried on the beautiful island.

Name _____

Reading Skills

1. What island could you see in Rhode Island?

    _____Block Island

    _____Kidd Island

    _____Watch Island

2. Rhode Island is the _____ state.

   smallest largest prettiest

3. Rhode Island has a nickname. It is
    _____Little Rhody. _____Bay State. _____Pirate State.

Word Play

1. Write one other word that you can make from the word
   Rhode Island. Answer: _____

2. Write a word that starts with the letters *bl*. _____

3. If you take a _____ you can get to Block Island.

   boat rocket

Thinking Further

1. Would you want to travel to Block Island? Why or why not?

2. Give Rhode Island another nickname.

Directions:
Reading Skills–Comprehension and Facts and Details (1-3): Have students read the question and mark the correct answer.
Word Play (1-3): Have students read each question carefully and then write their answer or answers on the lines provided. Word play questions will include the following: rhyming words, missing letters, finding words, picture clues, and using the correct word.
Thinking Further (1-2): Have students read each question and then discuss their responses, or have them write down their thoughts on a separate sheet of paper.

Vermont

Vermont gets its name from two French words. *Vert* means *green* and *mont* means *mountain*. Vermont is known as the "Green Mountain" state. If you go to Vermont you should see a sugarhouse. A sugarhouse is where maple tree sap is turned into maple syrup. Try some on your pancakes. You can also hike up the Bread Loaf Mountain. This mountain looks like a green loaf of bread!

Name _____

Reading Skills

1. What might you see if you live in Vermont?

    _____green mountains

    _____blue mountains

    _____green rivers

2. You can climb _____Bread Loaf Mountain. _____Butter Mountain. _____Meatloaf Mountain.

3. Maple tree sap is turned into syrup. This happens in a _____milk house. _____sugarhouse. _____sap house.

Word Play

1. Write one other word that you can make from the word *Vermont*. _____

2. Write one other word that rhymes with *green*. _____.

3. Syrup tastes _____.

    sweet sour

Thinking Further

1. Would you want to live in Vermont? Why or why not?

Directions:
Reading Skills–Comprehension and Facts and Details (1-3): Have students read the question and mark the correct answer.
Word Play (1-3): Have students read each question carefully and then write their answer or answers on the lines provided. Word play questions will include the following: rhyming words, missing letters, finding words, picture clues, and using the correct word.
Thinking Further (1): Have students read each question and then discuss their responses, or have them write down their thoughts on a separate sheet of paper.

Kentucky

President Lincoln was born in Kentucky. He went to a log cabin school when he was a boy.

Kentucky is also the home of the Kentucky Derby. This is a famous horse race. Every May, horses race against each other.

In Kentucky, you can see the longest cave in the world. The cave has an underground river! You can take a boat trip down this dark river.

Name _____

Reading Skills

1. What horse race takes place in Kentucky?

_____Kentucky Derby

_____Kentucky Doggie

_____Kansas Derby

2. President _____ was born in Kentucky.
Lincoln Kennedy Washington

3. Kentucky has the longest _____ in the world.
cave wave

Word Play

1. Write one other word that you can make from the word *Kentucky*. _____

2. Write one other word that rhymes with *log*. _____.

Thinking Further

1. Do you like horses? Would you want to see a race? Why or why not?

2. Give Kentucky a nickname.

Directions:
Reading Skills–Comprehension and Facts & Details (1-3): Have students read the question and mark the correct answer.
Word Play (1-2): Have students read each question carefully and then write their answer or answers on the lines provided. Word play questions will include the following: rhyming words, missing letters, finding words, picture clues, and using the correct word.
Thinking Further (1-2): Have students read each question and then discuss their responses, or have them write down their thoughts on a separate sheet of paper.

Connecticut

Connecticut is the birthplace of Noah Webster. Noah published the first American dictionary in 1806. Noah was born in West Hartford, Connecticut. He lived in a red saltbox house. In the winter, it was very cold. His family would sit around the huge brick fireplace in the kitchen. They would read by candlelight.

Today, Noah's old house is a museum. Many people visit all year. Spelling bees are held at his house. If you visit during a town spelling bee party you can bob for apples and play with cornhusk dolls.

Name _____

Reading Skills

1. Noah Webster grew up in

_____West Hartford.

_____East Hartford.

_____West Hattyfields.

2. He lived in a _____ saltbox house.
    black brown red

Word Play

1. Write one other word that you can make from the word
Noah. _____

2. Write one word that rhymes with *west*. _____

3. I will _____ six years old on June 10th.
    be buy bee

Thinking Further

1. Would you want to meet Noah Webster? Why or why not?

2. Would you want to write a dictionary?

Directions:
Reading Skills–Comprehension and Facts and Details (1-2): Have students read the question and mark the correct answer.
Word Play (1-3): Have students read each question carefully and then write their answer or answers on the lines provided. Word play questions will include the following: rhyming words, missing letters, finding words, picture clues, and using the correct word.
Thinking Further (1-2): Have students read each question and then discuss their responses, or have them write down their thoughts on a separate sheet of paper.

New Hampshire

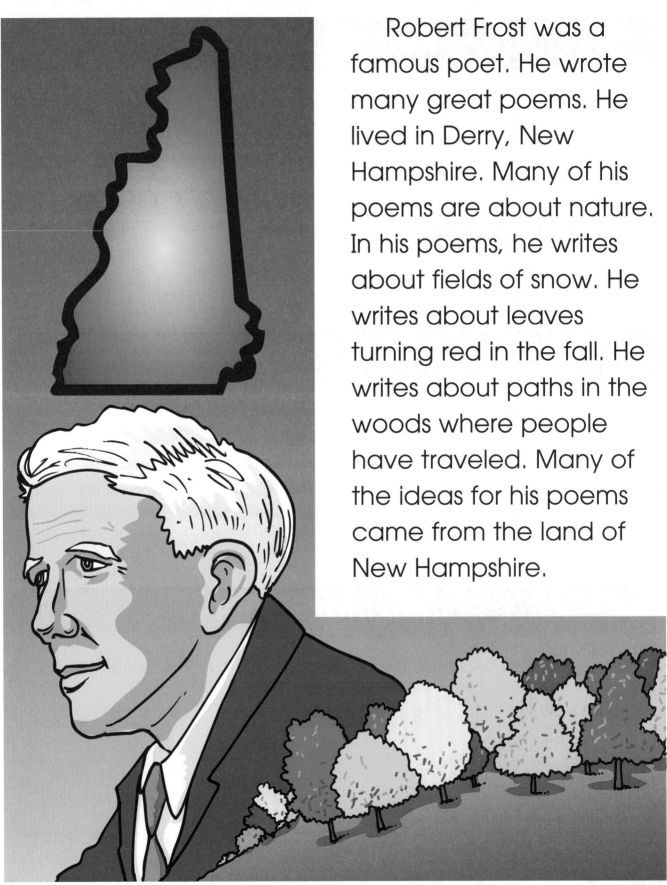

Robert Frost was a famous poet. He wrote many great poems. He lived in Derry, New Hampshire. Many of his poems are about nature. In his poems, he writes about fields of snow. He writes about leaves turning red in the fall. He writes about paths in the woods where people have traveled. Many of the ideas for his poems came from the land of New Hampshire.

Name _____

Reading Skills

1. Robert Frost was a famous

   _____song writer.

   _____poet.

   _____singer.

Poems

2. Many of his poems are about _____roses. _____buildings. _____nature.

3. What do you think Robert Frost would rather write a poem about?
   _____bikes _____trees _____trucks

Word Play

1. Write one other word that you can make from the word
   New Hampshire. _____

2. Write one other word that rhymes with *fall.* _____

3. In New Hampshire, the _____ is pretty.
   land lend

Thinking Further

1. Would you want to live in New Hampshire? Why or why not?

2. What would you like to write a poem about?

Directions:
Reading Skills–Comprehension and Facts and Details (1-3): Have students read the question and mark the correct answer.
Word Play (1-3): Have students read each question carefully and then write their answer or answers on the lines provided. Word play questions will include the following: rhyming words, missing letters, finding words, picture clues, and using the correct word.
Thinking Further (1-2): Have students read each question and then discuss their responses, or have them write down their thoughts on a separate sheet of paper.

Wisconsin

There are many dairy farmers in the state of Wisconsin. Dairy farmers make cheese, milk, and butter.

In fact, one of the largest hunks of cheese ever made came from here. "The Belle of Wisconsin" was a 40,060-pound Cheddar cheese. This hunk of cheese was so big it could make 300,000 grilled cheese sandwiches!

"The Belle of Wisconsin" toured America in a special car called the "Cheesemobile." It was sliced up and sold in 1989.

Name _____

Reading Skills

1. There are many _____ in Wisconsin.

_____teachers

_____dairy farmers

_____cowboys

2. Dairy farmers make _____orange juice. _____cheese. _____cookies.

Word Play

1. Write one other word that you can make from the word *Wisconsin.* _____

2. Write one other word that rhymes with *in.* _____

3. Dairy farmers make _____ to drink.
mill milk mud

Thinking Further

1. Would you want to live in Wisconsin? Why or why not?

2. Would you want to tour America in the "Cheesemobile"?

Directions:
Reading Skills–Comprehension and Facts and Details (1-2): Have students read the question and mark the correct answer.
Word Play (1-3): Have students read each question carefully and then write their answer or answers on the lines provided. Word play questions will include the following: rhyming words, missing letters, finding words, picture clues, and using the correct word.
Thinking Further (1-2): Have students read each question and then discuss their responses, or have them write down their thoughts on a separate sheet of paper.

Montana

Montana is called "Big Sky Country." The big, blue sky seems to meet the land. One thing to visit here is Grasshopper Glacier. Millions of grasshoppers are frozen in the glacier ice for you to see.

Montana has more than 50 mountain ranges. Rocky Mountain goats call the rocks home. These white and furry goats can walk on sharp rocks. The goats are hard to see because they live so high up on the rocks.

Name _____

Reading Skills

1. Montana is called

   _____ "Big Time."

   _____ "Big Sky Country."

   _____ "Big Cow."

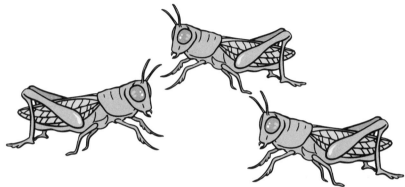

2. Grasshopper Glacier has _____ of frozen grasshoppers.

   _____ a couple _____ hundreds _____ millions

Word Play

1. Write one other word that you can make from the word
   Montana. _____

2. Write one other word that rhymes with *tan.* _____

3. The _____ sky is pretty in Montana.
   bed blue blew

Thinking Further

1. Would you want to live in Montana? Why or why not?

2. Which would you want to see more, a grasshopper, glacier, or a
   Rocky Mountain goat? Explain why.

Directions:
Reading Skills–Comprehension and Facts and Details (1-2): Have students read the question and mark the correct answer.
Word Play (1-3): Have students read each question carefully and then write their answer or answers on the lines provided. Word play questions will include the following: rhyming words, missing letters, finding words, picture clues, and using the correct word.
Thinking Further (1-2): Have students read each question and then discuss their responses, or have them write down their thoughts on a separate sheet of paper.

Nevada

Nevada is the driest state in the United States. It has many human-made lakes. These lakes help bring water to the land. Two places you might want to visit here are a lake and a dam.

Lake Tahoe is a beautiful lake. It has snowy mountains all around it. It also has some of the clearest water.

Hoover Dam was named after the 31st president. Huge piles of cement were used to make the dam strong. The same amount of cement could be used to build a highway from New York City all the way to San Francisco!

Name _____

Reading Skills

1. Nevada is the _____ state in the United States.

____rainiest

____driest

____hottest

2. Huge piles of cement were used to make Hoover Dam _____strong. _____gray. _____cold.

Word Play

1. Write one other word that you can make from the word *state.* _____

2. Write one other word that rhymes with *at.* _____

3. Workers _____ cement to build the Hoover Dam.
us used was

Thinking Further

1. Would you want to live in Nevada? Why or why not?

2. Would you want to help build a giant water dam?

Texas

Texas is so big that is has two time zones. That means if you lived on one side of the state and Grandma lived on the other you wouldn't want to call too late!

Big Bend National Park in Texas is a great place to visit. It has more birds and bats than any other U.S. park. If you visit, you might see horned toads, armadillos, and prairie dogs. All roads in the park end at the Rio Grande River.

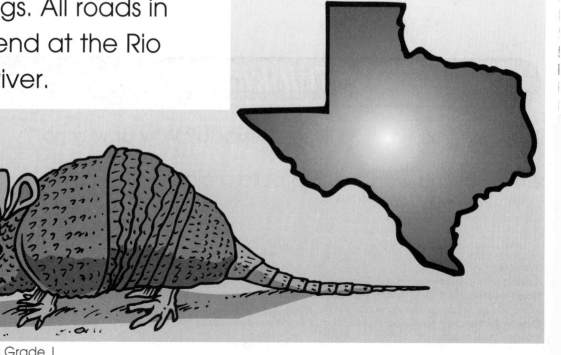

Name _____

Reading Skills

1. Texas is so big that is has _____ time zones.

_____three

_____two

_____one

2. If you visit Big Bend National Park, what might you see?
_____bats _____bears _____baboons

Word Play

1. Write one other word that you can make from the word
Texas. _____

2. Write one other word that rhymes with *big.* _____

3. I need to _____ Grandma on the phone.
cull call kall

Thinking Further

1. Would you want to live in Texas? Why or why not?

2. What animal would you most like to see?

Directions:
Reading Skills–Comprehension and Facts and Details (1-2): Have students read the question and mark the correct answer.
Word Play (1-3): Have students read each question carefully and then write their answer or answers on the lines provided. Word play questions will include the following: rhyming words, missing letters, finding words, picture clues, and using the correct word.
Thinking Further (1-2): Have students read each question and then discuss their responses, or have them write down their thoughts on a separate sheet of paper.

Hawaii

Hawaii is the 50th state. Over 100 islands make up Hawaii. New islands are still being made. These islands are made from volcanoes! Hawaii has black sand beaches also made from volcanoes.

The islands of Hawaii are in the middle of the Pacific Ocean. Some plants and animals found on Hawaii cannot be seen anywhere else.

If you visit Hawaii, you can visit a volcano. You can visit a black sand beach. When you get off the plane, people will say *Aloha*. *Aloha* is how people welcome you in Hawaii. *Aloha* also means *love*.

Reading Skills

1. Over _____ islands make up Hawaii.

   _____one hundred

   _____two hundred

   _____three hundred

2. The word *Aloha* means

   _____*like.* _____*pretty.* _____*love.*

Word Play

1. Write one other word that you can make from the word
   black. _____

2. Write one other word that rhymes with *say.* _____

3. Hawaii has _____ sand beaches.
   blue black brown

Thinking Further

1. Would you want to live in Hawaii? Why or why not?

2. Would you want to tour a volcano?

Directions:
Reading Skills–Comprehension and Facts and Details (1-2): Have students read the question and mark the correct answer.
Word Play (1-3): Have students read each question carefully and then write their answer or answers on the lines provided. Word play questions will include the following: rhyming words, missing letters, finding words, picture clues, and using the correct word.
Thinking Further (1-2): Have students read each question and then discuss their responses, or have them write down their thoughts on a separate sheet of paper.

Maryland

Maryland is known as "mini America." Here, you can see bays. You can see valleys. Maryland has beaches. Maryland has mountains, too.

If you visit this state, you can take a boat ride on the bay. You can visit the harbor where Francis Scott Key wrote a famous song. He was on a boat when he wrote the national anthem for America. Maryland has things for everybody to do.

Name _____

Reading Skills

1. What might you see in Maryland?

    _____bays

    _____a rain forest

    _____the tallest mountain

2. Maryland has things to do for _____everybody. _____a few people.

Word Play

1. What is a word that rhymes with *Mary*? _____

2. What is one other word you can make from the letters in *Maryland*? _____

3. What letter is missing from this sentence? Maryland is a ___un state.

Thinking Further

1. Would you like to live in Maryland? Why or why not?

2. What would you nickname Maryland?

Directions:
Reading Skills—Comprehension and Facts and Details (1-2): Have students read the question and mark the correct answer.
Word Play (1-3): Have students read each question carefully and then write their answer or answers on the lines provided. Word play questions will include the following: rhyming words, missing letters, finding words, picture clues, and using the correct word.
Thinking Further (1-2): Have students read each question and then discuss their responses, or have them write down their thoughts on a separate sheet of paper.

California

California is the state with the most people in it. It is the third largest state.

This is a state where you can ski on a mountain. A few hours later, you can swim in the sea! In this state, you can see Redwood forests and huge deserts.

This is a state where lots of movies are made. Many computer games are created here, too. This is a fun state to visit.

Name _____

Reading Skills

1. What might you see in California?

_____ movie making

_____ kangaroos

_____ cornfields

2. Why do so many people visit California?

_____ There are many pretty places to visit.

_____ There are lots of cars.

_____ There are lots of people.

Word Play

1. What is a word that rhymes with *lots*? _____

2. What is one other word you can make from the letters in *California*? _____

3. What letters are missing from this sentence?
California is a sun___y state.

Thinking Further

1. Would you like to live in California? Why or why not?

2. What would you nickname California?

Directions:

Reading Skills—Comprehension and Facts and Details (1-2): Have students read the question and mark the correct answer.

Word Play (1-3): Have students read each question carefully and then write their answer or answers on the lines provided. Word play questions will include the following: rhyming words, missing letters, finding words, picture clues, and using the correct word.

Thinking Further (1-2): Have students read each question and then discuss their responses, or have them write down their thoughts on a separate sheet of paper.

Florida

Come to Florida and see orange trees and beaches. You might even see some alligators.

Florida is also home to Cape Canaveral, where many spaceships are launched.

Florida often is very warm and sunny. Yet, in late summer, hurricanes often take place. Hurricanes have people's first names, such as Alex, Gloria, and Andrew.

Name _____

Reading Skills

1. What might you see in Florida?

   _____polar bears

   _____alligators

   _____bears

2. What fruit is grown a lot in Florida?

   _____bananas _____apples _____oranges

Word Play

1. What is another word that begins with *fl*? _____

2. What is one word you can make from the letters in *hurricane*? _____

Thinking Further

1. Would you like to live in Florida? Why or why not?

2. What would nickname the state of Florida?

Directions:
Reading Skills—Comprehension and Facts and Details (1-2): Have students read the question and mark the correct answer.
Word Play (1-2): Have students read each question carefully and then write their answer or answers on the lines provided. Word play questions will include the following: rhyming words, missing letters, finding words, picture clues, and using the correct word.
Thinking Further (1-2): Have students read each question and then discuss their responses, or have them write down their thoughts on a separate sheet of paper.

New York

Visit the state of New York and you will see rivers and busy cities. New York is the state where many people came first when moving to America.

New York City has more people than any other U.S. city. It has huge buildings. It has Broadway shows. It has yummy places to eat. New York City is also the home for the Statue of Liberty.

Name _____

Reading Skills

1. What might you see in New York?

   _____Statue of Liberty

   _____Statue of Freedom

   _____Painting of Liberty

2. Why might it be fun to visit New York City?

   _____There are a lot of fun things to do.

   _____It is sunny.

   _____There are a lot of roads.

Word Play

1. What are three words that rhyme with *top*? _____

2. What is one word you can make from the word *skyscraper*? _____

Thinking Further

1. Would you like to visit New York? Why or why not?

2. What would you nickname New York?

Directions:
Reading Skills—Comprehension and Facts and Details (1-2): Have students read the question and mark the correct answer.
Word Play (1-2): Have students read each question carefully and then write their answer or answers on the lines provided. Word play questions will include the following: rhyming words, missing letters, finding words, picture clues, and using the correct word.
Thinking Further (1-2): Have students read each question and then discuss their responses, or have them write down their thoughts on a separate sheet of paper.

Pennsylvania

Pennsylvania was named after William Penn. Pennsylvania has lots of green valleys and farmland.

It is home to two big cities, Pittsburgh and Philadelphia. Philadelphia is where many important papers were signed for America. The Declaration of Independence was signed there. In Philadelphia, you can see the Liberty Bell, too.

Name _____

Reading Skills

1. What might you see in Pennsylvania?

   _____Liberty Bell

   _____Statue of Liberty

   _____Liberty Well

2. Philadelphia is a city where famous people signed
   _____baseball cards. _____important papers. _____art.

Word Play

1. What is one word that rhymes with *bell*? _____

2. What is one word you can make from the letters in
   Pennsylvania? _____

Thinking Further

1. Would you learn a lot by going to Philadelphia? Why or why not?

2. What are two words to describe Pennsylvania?

Directions:
Reading Skills—Comprehension and Facts and Details (1-2): Have students read the question and mark the correct answer.
Word Play (1-2): Have students read each question carefully and then write their answer or answers on the lines provided. Word play questions will include the following: rhyming words, missing letters, finding words, picture clues, and using the correct word.
Thinking Further (1-2): Have students read each question and then discuss their responses, or have them write down their thoughts on a separate sheet of paper.

South Dakota

Can you imagine seeing four huge faces carved into the side of a mountain? What if these faces were four of our presidents? Wow! Well, you can see this at Mt. Rushmore in South Dakota.

You can also see the Badlands. Is this bad land? No! It is land full of gorges and mesas. You can also see the Black Hills. These hills look dark from far away.

Reading Skills

1. Mount Rushmore has _____ faces carved out of stone.

_____ three

_____ two

_____ four

2. The Badlands are _____ bad. _____ good. _____ filled with gorges.

Word Play

1. What is one word that rhymes with *south*? Look at the picture for a clue. _____

2. What is one word you can make from the letters in *Badlands*? _____

3. The Black Hills look _____ from far away.

dark   dim   silly

Thinking Further

1. Would you want to see Mount Rushmore? Why or why not?

2. Do you think it would be hard to carve people's heads out of stone?

Directions:
Reading Skills—Comprehension and Facts and Details (1-2): Have students read the question and mark the correct answer.
Word Play (1-2): Have students read each question carefully and then write their answer or answers on the lines provided. Word play questions will include the following: rhyming words, missing letters, finding words, picture clues, and using the correct word.
Thinking Further (1-2): Have students read each question and then discuss their responses, or have them write down their thoughts on a separate sheet of paper.

Virginia

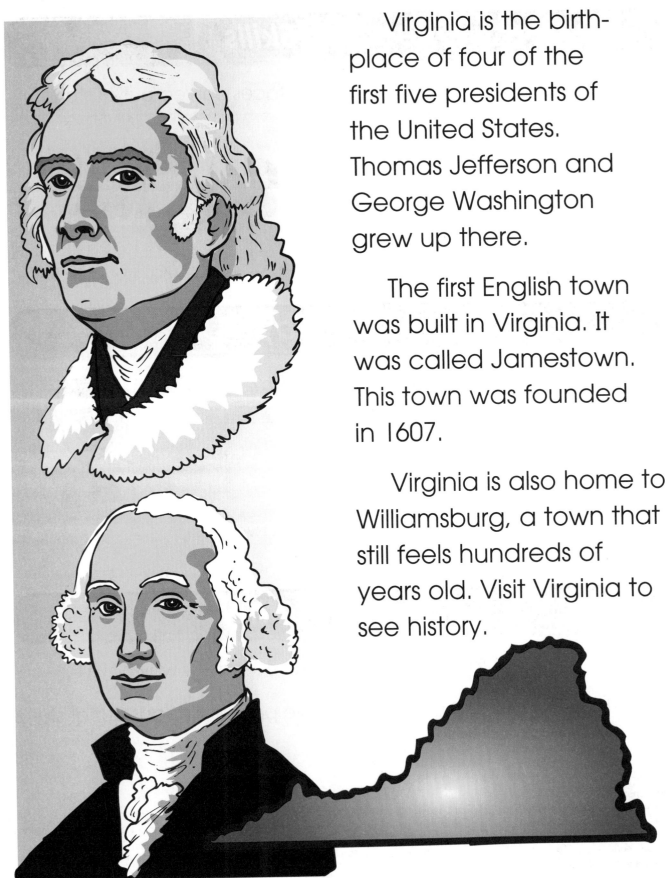

Virginia is the birthplace of four of the first five presidents of the United States. Thomas Jefferson and George Washington grew up there.

The first English town was built in Virginia. It was called Jamestown. This town was founded in 1607.

Virginia is also home to Williamsburg, a town that still feels hundreds of years old. Visit Virginia to see history.

Name _____

Reading Skills

1. What president was born in Virginia?

   _____George Washington

   _____George Bush

   _____King George

2. What was the name of the first English town?

   _____Jamestown _____Jimstown

Word Play

1. What is one word that rhymes with *town*? _____

2. George Washington grew _____ in Virginia as a boy.

up down around

3. The first English _____ was built in Virginia.

park town barn

Thinking Further

1. Would you like to visit Virginia? Why or why not?

2. What do you think you might see in an old-fashioned town like Williamsburg?

Directions:

Reading Skills—Comprehension and Facts and Details (1-2): Have students read the question and mark the correct answer.

Word Play (1-3): Have students read each question carefully and then write their answer or answers on the lines provided. Word play questions will include the following: rhyming words, missing letters, finding words, picture clues, and using the correct word.

Thinking Further (1-2): Have students read each question and then discuss their responses, or have them write down their thoughts on a separate sheet of paper.

Minnesota

It is freezing cold! Winters in Minnesota can be so cold that wet hair turns to ice. Bundle up!

The summers are warm. You can go fishing or boating. You can swim in many of the state's thousands of lakes.

Minnesota is also home to two big cities. These cities are next to each other. They are Minneapolis and St. Paul. These two cities are known as the "Twin Cities."

Reading Skills

1. Winters in Minnesota can be so cold that wet hair turns to

_____snow.

_____ice.

_____dark.

2. Where might you go swimming in Minnesota?
_____lakes _____parks _____oceans

Word Play

1. What is one word that rhymes with *cold*? _____

2. What is one word you can make from the letters in *Minnesota*? _____

Thinking Further

1. Would you want to visit Minnesota? Why or why not?

2. What are two words that describe Minnesota?

Directions:
Reading Skills—Comprehension and Facts and Details (1-2): Have students read the question and mark the correct answer.
Word Play (1-2): Have students read each question carefully and then write their answer or answers on the lines provided. Word play questions will include the following: rhyming words, missing letters, finding words, picture clues, and using the correct word.
Thinking Further (1-2): Have students read each question and then discuss their responses, or have them write down their thoughts on a separate sheet of paper.

Colorado

Denver is the capital of Colorado. It is also a mile high up in the sky. It is called the "Mile High City."

Colorado is a state in the Rocky Mountains. Many people love to visit here to ski. Some people bike the mountain paths. Other people like to ride rafts in the wild rivers here.

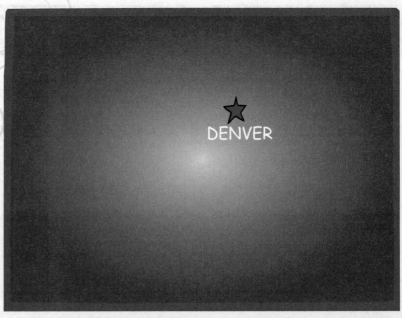

★
DENVER

Name _____

Reading Skills

1. The city of Denver is _____ in the sky.

_____low

_____high

_____blue

2. Some people come to this state to _____ski. _____surf. _____see fish.

Word Play

1. What is one word that rhymes with *it*? _____

2. What is one word you can make from the letters in *Colorado*? _____

Thinking Further

1. Would you like to ski, bike, or raft?

2. What are two words to describe Colorado?

Directions:
Reading Skills—Comprehension and Facts and Details (1-2): Have students read the question and mark the correct answer.
Word Play (1-2): Have students read each question carefully and then write their answer or answers on the lines provided. Word play questions will include the following: rhyming words, missing letters, finding words, picture clues, and using the correct word.
Thinking Further (1-2): Have students read each question and then discuss their responses, or have them write down their thoughts on a separate sheet of paper.

Arizona

Arizona is a great place. It is home to the Grand Canyon. This canyon is a wonder of the world. Millions of people visit it each year. They come to see its shapes and colors. Parts of the Grand Canyon are billions of years old!

If you visit the Grand Canyon, you might see fossils. You can camp overnight. Maybe you would want to ride a mule. Some people even raft down the river. Other people like to see the rocks from above. They take a plane ride and see the Canyon from high in the sky.

Name _____

Reading Skills

1. Why do people come to see the Grand Canyon?

   _____the sunshine

   _____the shapes of the rocks

   _____the food

2. What are some things you can do at the Grand Canyon?
   _____ look for fossils _____take a train ride _____make soap

Word Play

1. What is one word that rhymes with *ride*? _____

2. What is one word you can make from the word
   grand? _____

Thinking Further

1. Would you like to see the Grand Canyon? Why or why not?

2. What are two words to describe the Grand Canyon?

Directions:
Reading Skills—Comprehension and Facts and Details (1-2): Have students read the question and mark the correct answer.
Word Play (1-2): Have students read each question carefully and then write their answer or answers on the lines provided. Word play questions will include the following: rhyming words, missing letters, finding words, picture clues, and using the correct word.
Thinking Further (1-2): Have students read each question and then discuss their responses, or have them write down their thoughts on a separate sheet of paper.

Words to Know

1.   duck
dog
did

2.   for
fish
from

3.    grass
green
go

4.   bowl
bee
big

5.   call
can't
cold

6.   water
wet
won't

7.    pond
put
play

8.   foot
farm
for

9.   can
class
corn

10.   hop
hat
him

11.   road
run
red

12.   sun
son
sit

13.   pull
push
pail

14.   soft
set
says

15.   sleep
slip
sled

Directions:
Recognizing Familiar Words (1-15): Ask students to say the name of each picture and then circle the word that best describes the picture.

Spectrum Reading Grade 1

Words to Know

1.
snap
snail
snore

2.
has
hand
her

3.
pine
penny
pinch

4.
was
wing
wish

5.
fox
for
from

6.
dinner
dime
don't

7.
am
apple
ape

8.
want
wish
will

9.
whale
wink
what

10.
friend
feet
from

11.
fly
fry
fun

12.
sun
star
skip

13.
kit
kite
kiss

14.
gift
give
get

15.
string
step
skunk

Directions:
Recognizing Familiar Words (1-15): Ask students to say the name of each picture and then circle the word that best describes the picture.

Name _____

Contractions

can't   didn't

won't   let's

don't   that's

isn't   I'll

wasn't

1. do not _____

2. let us _____

3. will not _____

4. was not _____

5. is not _____

6. that is _____

7. can not _____

8. did not _____

9. I will _____

Directions:
Introducing Contractions (1-9): Explain the concept of contractions to students. Ask them to read aloud the contractions at the top of the page. Then, ask students to read the numbered pair of words. Next, have students write the correct contraction for the two words.

Lost Letters

1. Why does Little Duck want to fly?

   He wants to see the blue s____y.

2. How can he fly?

   With his w____ngs.

3. Do boys and girls have wings?

   N____t that I can se____.

4. Do fish have wings?

   N____, but they have f____ns.

5. Can Little Duck dive?

   Yes, he can d____ve.

Directions:

Missing Letters (1-5): Have students read each sentence and fill in the missing letters.

Lost Letters

1. What animal did Carolyn pick?

She picked a k____tten.

2. How did the kitten feel?

The new kitten felt s____ft.

3. What kind of pets do most people have?

Most people have c____ts or d____gs.

4. Do some people have different pets?

Max has a pet fr____g and a pet t____rtle.

5. Would a tiger make a good pet?

No, a tiger wo____'t make a good pet.

Directions:
Missing Letters (1-5): Have students read each sentence and fill in the missing letters.

Name _____

Words to Know

1.
   hall
   home
   hop

2.
   bear
   bee
   big

3.
   pat
   pet
   pit

4.
   green
   great
   good

5.
   bench
   boat
   belt

6.
   like
   love
   log

7. **2**
   to
   two
   toe

8.
   bend
   back
   bath

9.
   big
   bring
   bow

10.
    bars
    bug
    birds

11.
    call
    can't
    can

12.
    land
    lick
    lip

13.
    can
    cage
    call

14.
    play
    pan
    pin

15.
    ran
    run
    rock

Directions:
Recognizing familiar words (1-15): Ask students to say the name of each picture and then circle the word that best describes the picture.

Answer Key

3

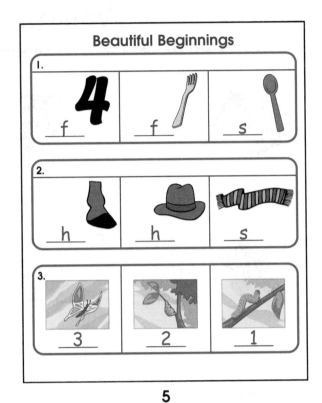

5

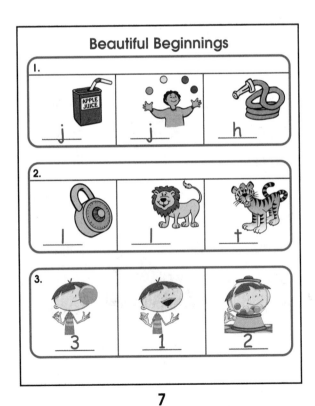

7

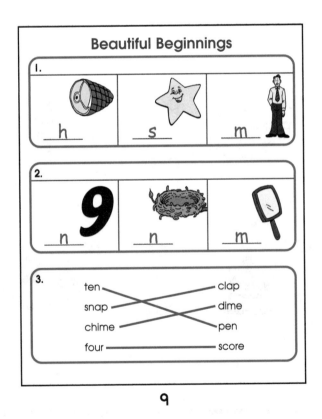

9

Answer Key

11

Beautiful Beginnings

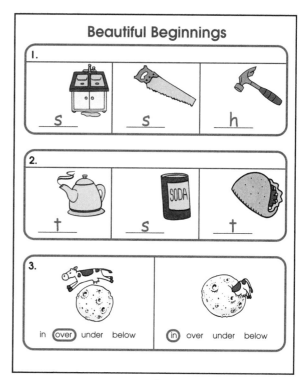

1. s   s   h

2. t   s   t

3. in (over) under below   (in) over under below

13

Exceptional Endings and Blends

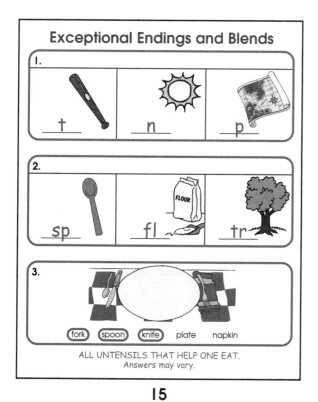

1. t   n   p

2. sp   fl   tr

3. (fork) (spoon) (knife) plate napkin

ALL UNTENSILS THAT HELP ONE EAT.
Answers may vary.

15

Exceptional Endings and Blends

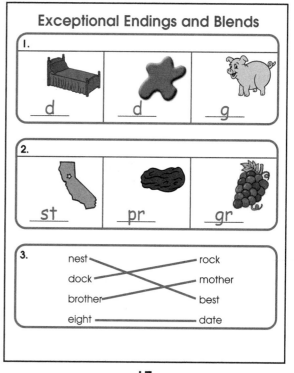

1. d   d   g

2. st   pr   gr

3.
nest — best
dock — mother
brother — rock
eight — date

17

Answer Key

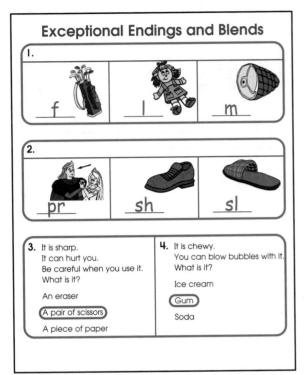

Exceptional Endings and Blends

1. f | l | m

2. pr | sh | sl

3. It is sharp.
It can hurt you.
Be careful when you use it.
What is it?

An eraser

(A pair of scissors)

A piece of paper

4. It is chewy.
You can blow bubbles with it.
What is it?

Ice cream

(Gum)

Soda

19

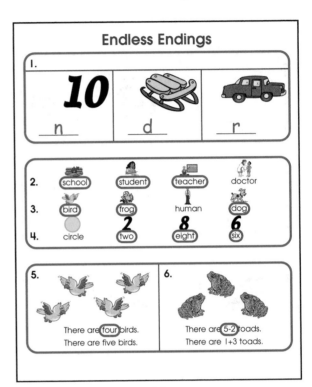

Endless Endings

1. **10** n | d | r

2. (school) (student) (teacher) doctor

3. (bird) (frog) human (dog)

4. circle **2** (two) **8** (eight) **6** (six)

5. There are (four) birds.
There are five birds.

6. There are (5-2) toads.
There are 1+3 toads.

21

More Endings

1. n | s | t

2. tr | fr | gr

3. Write a sentence that includes one of the words above in #2

Answers will vary. Example:
My grandfather has freckles.

23

Keep on Blending

1. g | n | r

2. fr | st | pr

3. 3 | 1 | 2

25

Answer Key

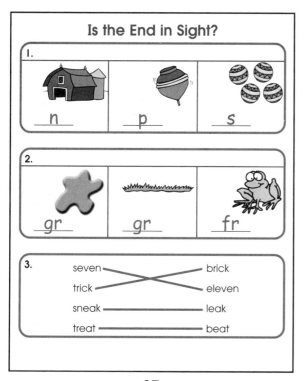

Is the End in Sight?

1. n   p   s

2. gr   gr   fr

3.
seven —— eleven
trick —— brick
sneak —— leak
treat —— beat

27

Valuable Vowels

1. a   e   i

2. ch   ch   ____

3. nickel, dime

29

Vowels

1. o   o   i

2. sh   sh   ____

3. fork, knife

31

Dynamite Digraphs

1. th   th   ____

2. a   u   o

3. Answers will vary.

33

Answer Key

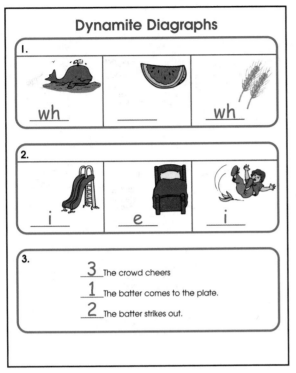

Dynamite Diagraphs

1.

wh | _____ | wh

2.

i | e | i

3.

_3_ The crowd cheers

_1_ The batter comes to the plate.

_2_ The batter strikes out.

35

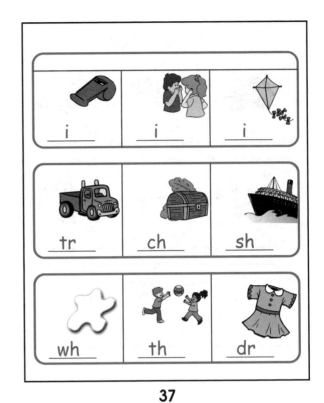

i | i | i

tr | ch | sh

wh | th | dr

37

Go Short or Go Long: A a

1. ate __long__
2. at __short__
3. ape __long__
4. act __short__
5. ant __short__
6. age __long__
7. rake __long__
8. ray __long__
9. able __long__
10. rat __short__
11. rack __short__
12. rate __long__
13. Andy __short__
14. Alex __short__
15. Abe __long__

39

Go Short or Go Long: E e

1. pen __short__
2. pencil __short__
3. plea __long__
4. pea __long__
5. glee __long__
6. green __long__
7. tea __long__
8. ten __short__
9. teen __long__
10. hen __short__
11. fence __short__
12. bee __long__
13. be __long__
14. bend __short__
15. Ben __short__

green

41

Answer Key

Go Short or Go Long: I i

1. pie __long__
2. pin __short__
3. pine __long__
4. pink __short__
5. pit __short__
6. tin __short__
7. time __long__
8. tiny __long__
9. tick __short__
10. Tim __short__
11. die __long__
12. dim __short__
13. diet __long__
14. dine __long__
15. dinner __short__

43

Go Short or Go Long: O o

1. pot __short__
2. spot __short__
3. snow __long__
4. not __short__
5. oat __long__
6. on __short__
7. box __short__
8. mop __short__
9. rope __long__
10. Oliver __short__
11. show __long__
12. shop __short__
13. clock __short__
14. stop __short__
15. slope __long__

45

Go Short or Go Long: U u

1. under __short__
2. cube __long__
3. umbrella __short__
4. cut __short__
5. cute __long__
6. butter __short__
7. yummy __short__
8. mule __long__
9. club __short__
10. duck __short__
11. dune __long__
12. tuck __short__
13. tune __long__
14. run __short__
15. funny __short__

47

Big Time Rhyme

1. funny
2. honey
3. duck
4. stop
5. ton
6. snow
7. bear
8. spring
9. fall
10. tell
11. tear

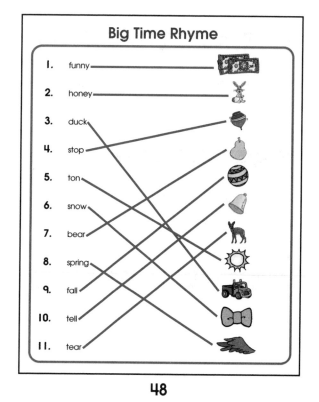

48

Answer Key

Classified Information

1.	(sad)	(glad)	(mad)	cage	
2.	(five)	(alive)	(nine)	thirteen	
3.	(boat)	(don't)	(won't)	did	
4.	(wheat)	(seat)	(beat)	cat	
5.	(pie)	(pine)	pin	(spine)	
6.	jump	(true)	(cube)	(June)	
7.	(oat)	(coat)	spot	(moat)	
8.	(glee)	(green)	gem	(greet)	
9.	(hen)	(ten)	(tent)	teen	
10.	(ray)	rat	(rake)	(rate)	

49

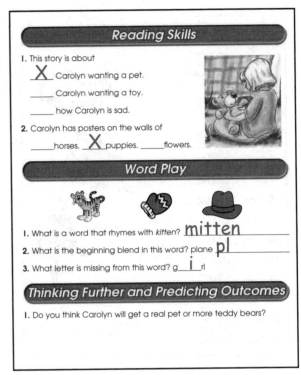

Reading Skills

1. This story is about

   X Carolyn wanting a pet.

   _____ Carolyn wanting a toy.

   _____ how Carolyn is sad.

2. Carolyn has posters on the walls of

   _____ horses. **X** puppies. _____ flowers.

Word Play

1. What is a word that rhymes with *kitten*? **mitten**
2. What is the beginning blend in this word? plane **pl**
3. What letter is missing from this word? g **i** rl

Thinking Further and Predicting Outcomes

1. Do you think Carolyn will get a real pet or more teddy bears?

51

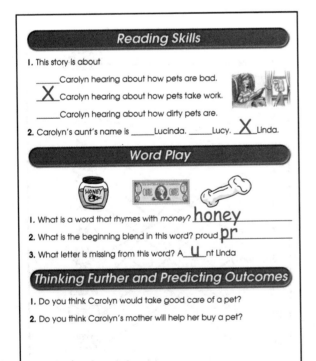

Reading Skills

1. This story is about

   _____ Carolyn hearing about how pets are bad.

   X Carolyn hearing about how pets take work.

   _____ Carolyn hearing about how dirty pets are.

2. Carolyn's aunt's name is _____ Lucinda. _____ Lucy. **X** Linda.

Word Play

1. What is a word that rhymes with *money*? **honey**
2. What is the beginning blend in this word? proud **pr**
3. What letter is missing from this word? A **u** nt Linda

Thinking Further and Predicting Outcomes

1. Do you think Carolyn would take good care of a pet?
2. Do you think Carolyn's mother will help her buy a pet?

53

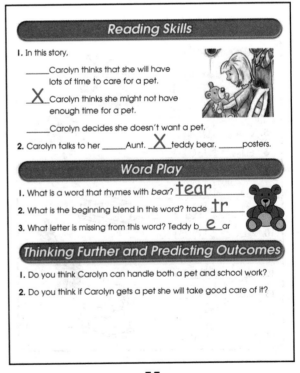

Reading Skills

1. In this story,

   _____ Carolyn thinks that she will have lots of time to care for a pet.

   X Carolyn thinks she might not have enough time for a pet.

   _____ Carolyn decides she doesn't want a pet.

2. Carolyn talks to her _____ Aunt. **X** teddy bear. _____ posters.

Word Play

1. What is a word that rhymes with *bear*? **tear**
2. What is the beginning blend in this word? trade **tr**
3. What letter is missing from this word? Teddy b **e** ar

Thinking Further and Predicting Outcomes

1. Do you think Carolyn can handle both a pet and school work?
2. Do you think if Carolyn gets a pet she will take good care of it?

55

Answer Key

Reading Skills

1. In this story,

_____ Carolyn's dad tells her she can't have a pet.

__X__ Carolyn's dad talks about other types of pets.

_____ Carolyn's dad says he will buy her a dog.

2. Carolyn's dad mentions a possible pet. It is a

__X__ turtle. _____ bunny. _____ pony.

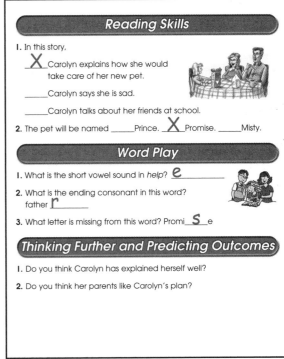

Word Play

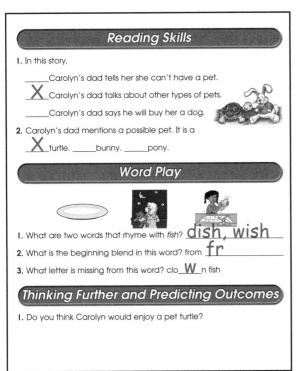

1. What are two words that rhyme with *fish*? **dish, wish**

2. What is the beginning blend in this word? from **fr**

3. What letter is missing from this word? clo__W__n fish

Thinking Further and Predicting Outcomes

1. Do you think Carolyn would enjoy a pet turtle?

57

Reading Skills

1. In this story,

__X__ Carolyn explains how she would take care of her new pet.

_____ Carolyn says she is sad.

_____ Carolyn talks about her friends at school.

2. The pet will be named _____ Prince. __X__ Promise. _____ Misty.

Word Play

1. What is the short vowel sound in *help*? **e**

2. What is the ending consonant in this word? father **r**

3. What letter is missing from this word? Promi__s__e

Thinking Further and Predicting Outcomes

1. Do you think Carolyn has explained herself well?

2. Do you think her parents like Carolyn's plan?

59

Reading Skills

1. This story is about

__X__ Carolyn waking up early to find out if she will get a pet.

_____ Carolyn waking up early to go to school.

_____ Carolyn sleeping because she is so tired.

2. Carolyn's last name is __X__ Jones. _____ Promise. _____ Linda.

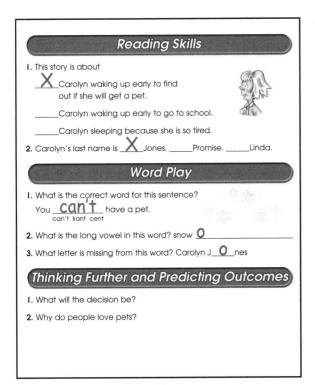

Word Play

1. What is the correct word for this sentence?

You **can't** have a pet.
can't kant cent

2. What is the long vowel in this word? snow **o**

3. What letter is missing from this word? Carolyn J__o__nes

Thinking Further and Predicting Outcomes

1. What will the decision be?

2. Why do people love pets?

61

Reading Skills

1. This story is about

__X__ Carolyn finding out that she will get a pet.

_____ Carolyn finding out that she will not get a pet.

_____ Carolyn finding out she's late for school.

2. Carolyn hugged her _____ mother. _____ father. __X__ parents.

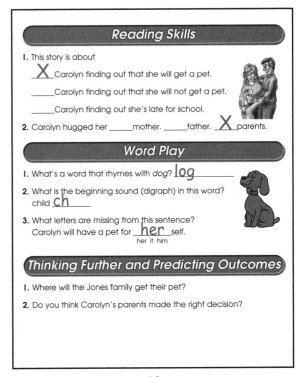

Word Play

1. What's a word that rhymes with *dog*? **log**

2. What is the beginning sound (digraph) in this word? child **ch**

3. What letters are missing from this sentence? Carolyn will have a pet for **her** self.
her it him

Thinking Further and Predicting Outcomes

1. Where will the Jones family get their pet?

2. Do you think Carolyn's parents made the right decision?

63

Answer Key

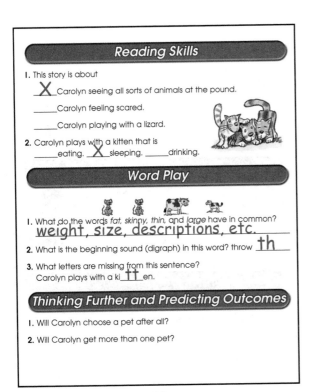

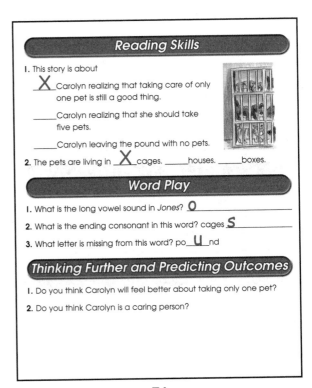

65

67

69

71

Answer Key

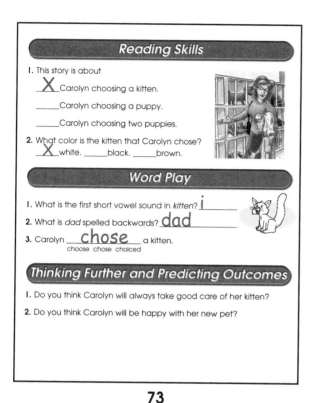

Reading Skills

1. This story is about

   X Carolyn choosing a kitten.

   _____ Carolyn choosing a puppy.

   _____ Carolyn choosing two puppies.

2. What color is the kitten that Carolyn chose?
   X white. _____ black. _____ brown.

Word Play

1. What is the first short vowel sound in *kitten*? **i** _____
2. What is *dad* spelled backwards? **dad** _____
3. Carolyn _____ **chose** _____ a kitten.
   choose   chose   choiced

Thinking Further and Predicting Outcomes

1. Do you think Carolyn will always take good care of her kitten?
2. Do you think Carolyn will be happy with her new pet?

73

Reading Skills

1. In this story,

   X Carolyn realizes she cannot have her kitten until tomorrow.

   _____ Carolyn learns that the kitten belongs to someone.

   _____ Carolyn learns that the kitten is 3 years old.

2. The kitten is a **X** boy. _____ girl.

Word Play

1. What is the short vowel sound in *shot*? **o** _____
2. What is the ending consonant in this word? shot **t** _____
3. What letter is missing from this word? cat fo **o** d

Thinking Further and Predicting Outcomes

1. Do you think Carolyn will be upset she can't have the kitten right away?
2. Do you think Carolyn will be nervous for the kitten because he needs a shot?

75

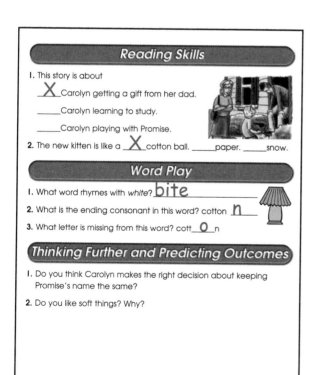

Reading Skills

1. This story is about

   X Carolyn getting a gift from her dad.

   _____ Carolyn learning to study.

   _____ Carolyn playing with Promise.

2. The new kitten is like a **X** cotton ball. _____ paper. _____ snow.

Word Play

1. What word rhymes with *white*? **bite** _____
2. What is the ending consonant in this word? cotton **n** _____
3. What letter is missing from this word? cott **o** n

Thinking Further and Predicting Outcomes

1. Do you think Carolyn makes the right decision about keeping Promise's name the same?
2. Do you like soft things? Why?

77

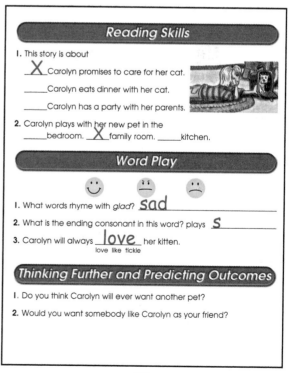

Reading Skills

1. This story is about

   X Carolyn promises to care for her cat.

   _____ Carolyn eats dinner with her cat.

   _____ Carolyn has a party with her parents.

2. Carolyn plays with her new pet in the
   _____ bedroom. **X** family room. _____ kitchen.

Word Play

1. What words rhyme with *glad*? **sad** _____
2. What is the ending consonant in this word? plays **s** _____
3. Carolyn will always _____ **love** _____ her kitten.
   love   like   tickle

Thinking Further and Predicting Outcomes

1. Do you think Carolyn will ever want another pet?
2. Would you want somebody like Carolyn as your friend?

79

Answer Key

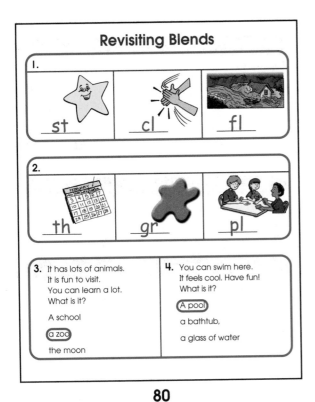

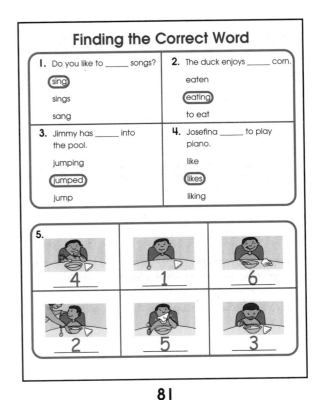

Answer Key

Where Are You?

1.

(next to) over above below | (in) over under below

2.

under (inside) around below | (outside) inside under below

3.

(in) next to around above | in beneath under (next to)

4.

down (up) sideways under | (down) up around near

84

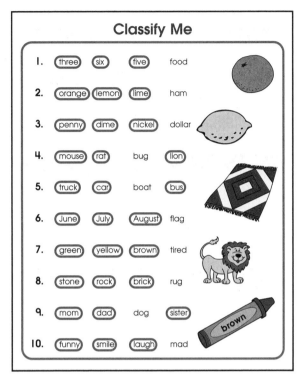

Classify Me

1. (three) (six) (five) food
2. (orange) (lemon) (lime) ham
3. (penny) (dime) (nickel) dollar
4. (mouse) (rat) bug (lion)
5. (truck) (car) boat (bus)
6. (June) (July) (August) flag
7. (green) (yellow) (brown) tired
8. (stone) (rock) (brick) rug
9. (mom) (dad) dog (sister)
10. (funny) (smile) (laugh) mad

85

Reading Skills

1. What might you see if you lived in Alaska?

_____ robins

__X__ moose

_____ lions

2. Alaska is __two times__ as big as Texas.
two times three times ten times

3. What did Joe Juneau search for in Alaska? ___Gold___
bears gold diamonds

Word Play

1. Write one other word that you can make from the word
Alaska. __Answers will vary.__

2. Write one other word that rhymes with bear. __Answers will__ vary.

3. If you __live__ in Alaska, you should own a hat.
live liked

Thinking Further

1. Would you want to live in Alaska? Why or why not?

2. What are a few words that describe Alaska?

87

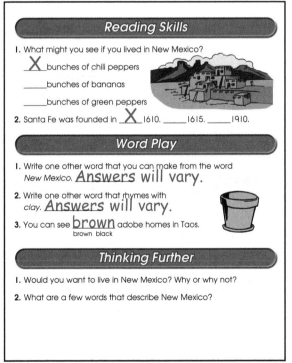

Reading Skills

1. What might you see if you lived in New Mexico?

__X__ bunches of chili peppers

_____ bunches of bananas

_____ bunches of green peppers

2. Santa Fe was founded in __X__1610. _____1615. _____1910.

Word Play

1. Write one other word that you can make from the word
New Mexico. __Answers will vary.__

2. Write one other word that rhymes with
clay. __Answers will vary.__

3. You can see __brown__ adobe homes in Taos.
brown black

Thinking Further

1. Would you want to live in New Mexico? Why or why not?

2. What are a few words that describe New Mexico?

89

Answer Key

Reading Skills

1. What might you see if you visited Oregon?

   X the deepest lake

   _____ the widest lake

   _____ the coldest lake

2. Some people went to Oregon because it had **rich** soil.

   rich poor dirty

Word Play

1. Write one other word that you can make from the word
   Oregon. **Answers will vary.**

2. Write one other word that rhymes with
   soil. **Answers will vary.**

3. Oregon is **cold** in the winter.

   cool cold

Thinking Further

1. Do you think there are farmers in Oregon? How do you know?

2. What are a few words that describe Oregon?

91

Reading Skills

1. What island could you see in Rhode Island?

   X Block Island

   _____ Kidd Island

   _____ Watch Island

2. Rhode Island is the **smallest** state.

   smallest largest prettiest

3. Rhode Island has a nickname. It is
   X Little Rhody. _____ Bay State. _____ Pirate State.

Word Play

1. Write one other word that you can make from the word
   Rhode Island. Answer: **Answers will vary.**

2. Write a word that starts with the letters *bl.* **Answers will vary.**

3. If you take a **boat** you can get to Block Island.

   boat rocket

Thinking Further

1. Would you want to travel to Block Island? Why or why not?

2. Give Rhode Island another nickname.

93

Reading Skills

1. What might you see if you live in Vermont?

   X green mountains

   _____ blue mountains

   _____ green rivers

2. You can climb **X** Bread Loaf Mountain. _____ Butter Mountain.
   _____ Meatloaf Mountain.

3. Maple tree sap is turned into syrup. This happens in a
   _____ milk house. **X** sugarhouse. _____ sap house.

Word Play

1. Write one other word that you can make from the word
   Vermont. **Answers will vary.**

2. Write one other word that rhymes with *green.* *Answers will vary.*

3. Syrup tastes **sweet**.

   sweet sour

Thinking Further

1. Would you want to live in Vermont? Why or why not?

95

Reading Skills

1. What horse race takes place in Kentucky?

   X Kentucky Derby

   _____ Kentucky Doggie

   _____ Kansas Derby

2. President **Lincoln** was born in Kentucky.

   Lincoln Kennedy Washington

3. Kentucky has the longest **cave** in the world.

   cave wave

Word Play

1. Write one other word that you can make from the word
   Kentucky. **Answers will vary.**

2. Write one other word that rhymes with *log.* **Answers will vary.**

Thinking Further

1. Do you like horses? Would you want to see a race?
   Why or why not?

2. Give Kentucky a nickname.

97

Answer Key

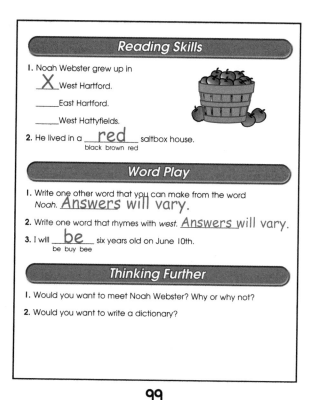

Reading Skills

1. Noah Webster grew up in
   __X__ West Hartford.
   _____ East Hartford.
   _____ West Hattyfields.

2. He lived in a ___red___ saltbox house.
   black brown red

Word Play

1. Write one other word that you can make from the word
   Noah. **Answers will vary.**

2. Write one word that rhymes with *west.* **Answers will vary.**

3. I will ___be___ six years old on June 10th.
   be buy bee

Thinking Further

1. Would you want to meet Noah Webster? Why or why not?

2. Would you want to write a dictionary?

99

Reading Skills

1. Robert Frost was a famous
   _____ song writer.
   __X__ poet.
   _____ singer.

2. Many of his poems are about _____ roses. _____ buildings. __X__ nature.

3. What do you think Robert Frost would rather write a poem about?
   _____ bikes __X__ trees _____ trucks

Word Play

1. Write one other word that you can make from the word
   New Hampshire. **Answers will vary.**

2. Write one other word that rhymes with *fall.* **Answers will vary.**

3. In New Hampshire, the ___land___ is pretty.
   land lend

Thinking Further

1. Would you want to live in New Hampshire? Why or why not?

2. What would you like to write a poem about?

101

Reading Skills

1. There are many _____ in Wisconsin.
   _____ teachers
   __X__ dairy farmers
   _____ cowboys

2. Dairy farmers make _____ orange juice. __X__ cheese.
   _____ cookies.

Word Play

1. Write one other word that you can make from the word
   Wisconsin. **Answers will vary.**

2. Write one other word that rhymes with *in.* **Answers will vary.**

3. Dairy farmers make ___milk___ to drink.
   mill milk mud

Thinking Further

1. Would you want to live in Wisconsin? Why or why not?

2. Would you want to tour America in the "Cheesemobile"?

103

Reading Skills

1. Montana is called
   _____ "Big Time."
   __X__ "Big Sky Country."
   _____ "Big Cow."

2. Grasshopper Glacier has _____ of frozen grasshoppers.
   _____ a couple _____ hundreds __X__ millions

Word Play

1. Write one other word that you can make from the word
   Montana. **Answers will vary.**

2. Write one other word that rhymes with *tan.* **Answers will vary.**

3. The ___blue___ sky is pretty in Montana.
   bed blue blew

Thinking Further

1. Would you want to live in Montana? Why or why not?

2. Which would you want to see more, a grasshopper, glacier, or a Rocky Mountain goat? Explain why.

105

Answer Key

Answer Key

Reading Skills

1. Nevada is the _____ state in the United States.
   - _____ rainiest
   - **X** driest
   - _____ hottest

2. Huge piles of cement were used to make Hoover Dam
   X strong. _____ gray. _____ cold.

Word Play

1. Write one other word that you can make from the word state. **Answers will vary.**

2. Write one other word that rhymes with *at*. **Answers will vary.**

3. Workers **used** cement to build the Hoover Dam.
   us used was

Thinking Further

1. Would you want to live in Nevada? Why or why not?

2. Would you want to help build a giant water dam?

107

Reading Skills

1. Texas is so big that is has _____ time zones.
   - _____ three
   - **X** two
   - _____ one

2. If you visit Big Bend National Park, what might you see?
   X bats _____ bears _____ baboons

Word Play

1. Write one other word that you can make from the word *Texas*. **Answers will vary.**

2. Write one other word that rhymes with *big*. **Answers will vary.**

3. I need to **call** Grandma on the phone.
   cull call kall

Thinking Further

1. Would you want to live in Texas? Why or why not?

2. What animal would you most like to see?

109

Reading Skills

1. Over _____ islands make up Hawaii.
   - **X** one hundred
   - _____ two hundred
   - _____ three hundred

2. The word *Aloha* means
   _____ like. _____ pretty. **X** love.

Word Play

1. Write one other word that you can make from the word *black*. **Answers will vary.**

2. Write one other word that rhymes with *say*. **Answers will vary.**

3. Hawaii has **black** sand beaches.
   blue black brown

Thinking Further

1. Would you want to live in Hawaii? Why or why not?

2. Would you want to tour a volcano?

111

Reading Skills

1. What might you see in Maryland?
   - **X** bays
   - _____ a rain forest
   - _____ the tallest mountain

2. Maryland has things to do for **X** everybody. _____ a few people.

Word Play

1. What is a word that rhymes with *Mary*? **Answers will vary.**

2. What is one other word you can make from the letters in *Maryland*? **Answers will vary.**

3. What letter is missing from this sentence? Maryland is a **f**un state.

Thinking Further

1. Would you like to live in Maryland? Why or why not?

2. What would you nickname Maryland?

113

Answer Key

Reading Skills

1. What might you see in California?

    X movie making

    _____ kangaroos

    _____ cornfields

2. Why do so many people visit California?

    X There are many pretty places to visit.

    _____ There are lots of cars.

    _____ There are lots of people.

Word Play

1. What is a word that rhymes with *lots*? **Answers will vary.**

2. What is one other word you can make from the letters in *California*? **Answers will vary.**

3. What letters are missing from this sentence?
California is a sun **n** y state.

Thinking Further

1. Would you like to live in California? Why or why not?

2. What would you nickname California?

115

Reading Skills

1. What might you see in Florida?

    _____ polar bears

    X alligators

    _____ bears

2. What fruit is grown a lot in Florida?

    _____ bananas _____ apples X oranges

Word Play

1. What is another word that begins with *fl*? **Answers will vary.**

2. What is one word you can make from the letters in *hurricane*? **Answers will vary.**

Thinking Further

1. Would you like to live in Florida? Why?

2. What would nickname the state of Florida?

117

Reading Skills

1. What might you see in New York?

    X Statue of Liberty

    _____ Statue of Freedom

    _____ Painting of Liberty

2. Why might it be fun to visit New York City?

    X There are a lot of fun things to do.

    _____ It is sunny.

    _____ There are a lot of roads.

Word Play

1. What are three words that rhyme with *top*? **Answers will vary.**

2. What is one word you can make from the word *skyscraper*? **Answers will vary.**

Thinking Further

1. Would you like to visit New York? Why?

2. What would you nickname New York?

119

Reading Skills

1. What might you see in Pennsylvania?

    X Liberty Bell

    _____ Statue of Liberty

    _____ Liberty Well

2. Philadelphia is a city where famous people signed
    _____ baseball cards. X important papers. _____ art.

Word Play

1. What is one word that rhymes with *bell*? **Answers will vary.**

2. What is one word you can make from the letters in *Pennsylvania*? **Answers will vary.**

Thinking Further

1. Would you learn a lot by going to Philadelphia? Why?

2. What are two words to describe Pennsylvania?

121

Answer Key

Reading Skills

1. Mount Rushmore has _____ faces carved out of stone.

   ____three

   ____two

   __X__four

2. The Badlands are ____bad. ____good. __X__filled with gorges.

Word Play

1. What is one word that rhymes with *south*? Look at the picture for a clue. <u>Answers will</u> vary.

2. What is one word you can make from the letters in *Badlands*? <u>Answers will vary.</u>

3. The Black Hills look <u>dark</u> from far away.
   dark dim silly

Thinking Further

1. Would you want to see Mount Rushmore? Why?

2. Do you think it would be hard to carve people's heads out of stone?

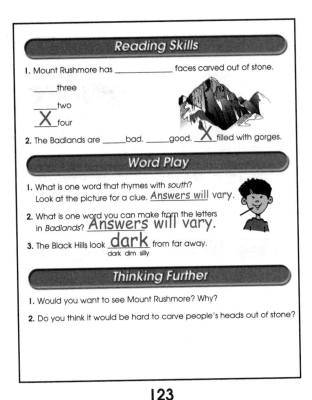

123

Reading Skills

1. What president was born in Virginia?

   __X__George Washington

   ____George Bush

   ____King George

2. What was the name of the first English town?
   __X__Jamestown ____Jimstown

Word Play

1. What is one word that rhymes with *town*? <u>Answers will vary.</u>

2. George Washington grew ___<u>up</u>___ in Virginia as a boy.
   up down around

3. The first English <u>town</u> was built in Virginia.
   park town barn

Thinking Further

1. Would you like to visit Virginia? Why or why not?

2. What do you think you might see in an old-fashioned town like Williamsburg?

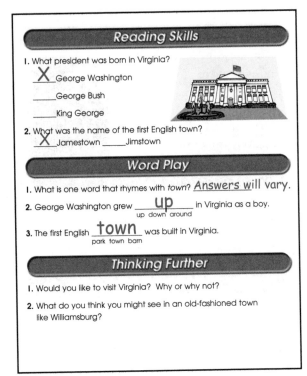

125

Reading Skills

1. Winters in Minnesota can be so cold that wet hair turns to

   ____snow.

   __X__ice.

   ____dark.

2. Where might you go swimming in Minnesota?
   __X__lakes ____parks ____oceans

Word Play

1. What is one word that rhymes with *cold*? <u>Answers will vary.</u>

2. What is one word you can make from the letters in *Minnesota*? <u>Answers will vary.</u>

Thinking Further

1. Would you want to visit Minnesota? Why?

2. What are two words that describe Minnesota?

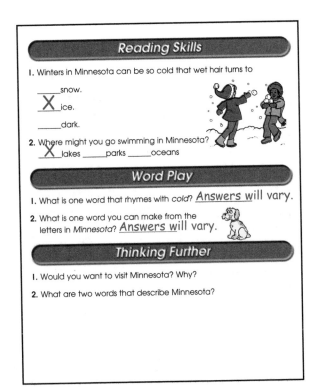

127

Reading Skills

1. The city of Denver is _____ in the sky.

   ____low

   __X__high

   ____blue

2. Some people come to this state to __X__ski. ____surf. ____see fish.

Word Play

1. What is one word that rhymes with *it*? <u>Answers will vary.</u>

2. What is one word you can make from the letters in *Colorado*? <u>Answers will vary.</u>

Thinking Further

1. Would you like to ski, bike, or raft?

2. What are two words to describe Colorado?

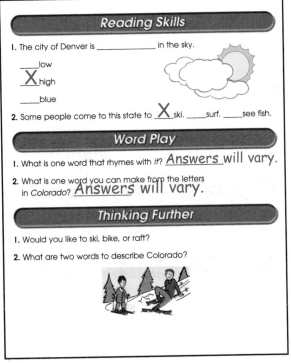

129

Answer Key

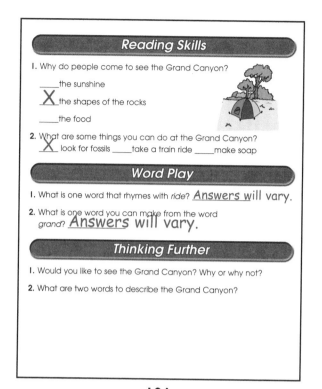

Reading Skills

1. Why do people come to see the Grand Canyon?

___ the sunshine

_X_ the shapes of the rocks

___ the food

2. What are some things you can do at the Grand Canyon?
_X_ look for fossils ___ take a train ride ___ make soap

Word Play

1. What is one word that rhymes with *ride*? **Answers will vary.**

2. What is one word you can make from the word *grand*? **Answers will vary.**

Thinking Further

1. Would you like to see the Grand Canyon? Why or why not?

2. What are two words to describe the Grand Canyon?

131

Words to Know

1. (duck) dog did
2. for (fish) from
3. (grass) green go
4. (bowl) bee big
5. call can't (cold)
6. (water) wet won't
7. (pond) put play
8. (foot) farm for
9. can class (corn)
10. hop (hat) him
11. (road) run red
12. (sun) son sit
13. pull push (pail)
14. (soft) set says
15. sleep slip (sled)

132

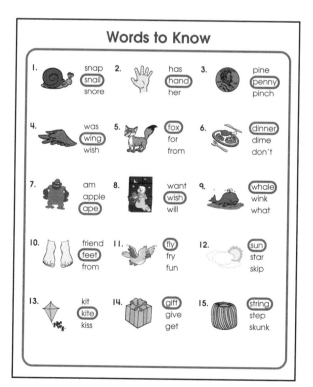

Words to Know

1. snap (snail) snore
2. has (hand) her
3. pine (penny) pinch
4. was (wing) wish
5. (fox) for from
6. (dinner) dime don't
7. am apple (ape)
8. want (wish) will
9. (whale) wink what
10. friend (feet) from
11. (fly) fry fun
12. (sun) star skip
13. kit (kite) kiss
14. (gift) give get
15. (string) step skunk

133

Contractions

can't didn't
won't let's
don't that's
isn't I'll
wasn't

1. do not **don't**
2. let us **let's**
3. will not **won't**
4. was not **wasn't**
5. is not **isn't**
6. that is **that's**
7. can not **can't**
8. did not **didn't**
9. I will **I'll**

134

Answer Key

Lost Letters

1. Why does Little Duck want to fly?

   He wants to see the blue s__k__y.

2. How can he fly?

   With his w__i__ngs.

3. Do boys and girls have wings?

   N__o__t that I can se__e__.

4. Do fish have wings?

   N__o__, but they have f__i__ns.

5. Can Little Duck dive?

   Yes, he can d__i__ve.

135

Lost Letters

1. What animal did Carolyn pick?

   She picked a k__i__tten.

2. How did the kitten feel?

   The new kitten felt s__o__ft.

3. What kind of pets do most people have?

   Most people have c__a__ts or d__o__gs.

4. Do some people have different pets?

   Max has a pet fr__o__g and a pet t__u__rtle.

5. Will a tiger make a good pet?

   No, a tiger wo__n__'t make a good pet.

136

Words to Know

1. hall / (home) / hop
2. (bear) / bee / big
3. pat / (pet) / pit
4. (green) / great / good
5. bench / (boat) / belt
6. like / (love) / log
7. **2** to / (two) / toe
8. bend / (back) / bath
9. big / bring / (bow)
10. (bars) / bug / birds
11. (call) / can't / can
12. (land) / lick / lip
13. can / (cage) / call
14. (play) / pan / pin
15. ran / run / (rock)

137

Notes

Notes